WALKING
THE CHURCH YEAR

Personal Devotions for
a Labyrinth Prayer Practice

ROBERT J. F. ELSNER

Church
PUBLISHING

Church Publishing
19 East 34th Street
New York, NY 10016

Cover design by Newgen
Cover image by iStock

Library of Congress Cataloging-in-Publication Data

Library of Congress Control Number: 2024930460

ISBN 978-1-64065-697-0 (paperback) | ISBN 978-1-64065-698-7 (ePUB)

This book is dedicated to
the Glory of God,
and to my Beloved wife, Betsy,
and to the parishioners
of the many Churches
at which I have served
in various capacities.
They have all served me far more
in giving me peace, love, and joy.

TABLE OF CONTENTS

PREFACE

T his book is not designed to teach you a particular way to journey through a labyrinth, but rather to help you as you develop your own feel and rhythm for it—with your *own* prayers and for your *own* needs. Labyrinths are representations of journeys, not just of the body, but of the mind, heart, and soul. Whether the journeys are to unknown countries, spiritual destinations, or new relationships with others, labyrinths are dynamic and involve change, especially as it pushes us to focus more on God.

Labyrinths are made to be walked, but not all of us are physically able to walk. For those of us so blessed, walking should be done at one's own pace, whether alone or with others, assisted by crutches, or held by helpers. For those who cannot walk, but are able to use a wheelchair, the same instructions apply. For those unable to do either, a printed or router-cut copy of a labyrinth can be used and followed with a finger or pointer. If a person is unable to see a printed labyrinth, one carved in wood, clay, or other material can be used or followed by feeling, as could outlining a labyrinth with dried school glue on paper.

If you have no access to a labyrinth, you can make one, either with objects in a room or yard, or create one in your mind in a public park using benches, trees, or even trash cans as places to turn. Be creative. Remember to focus on the benefits of the labyrinth, not the obstacles to doing the practice. Imagination is the basis of a labyrinth and should be nurtured in us all.

These meditations and journeys are not officially endorsed by any ecclesiastical body and are solely the creation of the author. While they are developed in an Anglican tradition, they borrow from many other Christian traditions. No endorsement or approval is implied from any specific governing body within the Church universal.

ORIGINS OF THIS BOOK

I have been walking labyrinths around the world since the 1960s. I was a kid in New York City and out on Long Island when the practice was revived, and it helped that my father, an Episcopal priest, loved the traditions of our faith and wanted my family and me to experience them.

As a young man studying at the École Le Cordon Bleu France, working as an embassy chef in London, and later pursuing a post-doctoral degree in Ireland, I walked countless labyrinths and mazes at great cathedrals and chateaux. I also helped plan and build labyrinths while I was serving at a few churches, opening them to communities beyond the High Church traditions that are most often associated with such practices.

I now attend Saint Stephen's Episcopal Church in Vestavia Hills, Alabama, which is known in our community as a warm, welcoming place that reaches out to help others in need. But tragedy struck this wonderful church in the summer of 2022, when a gunman opened fire in the parish hall and killed three of our parishioners.

The victims, Bart, Sharon, and Jane, were beautiful, kind-hearted people who had made me feel welcome when my family and I first joined the church. The congregants at Saint Stephen's and I were understandably heartbroken. How could our peaceful church be hit by such a senseless act of violence? Why did our wonderful friends have to die?

Despite my personal heartbreak, I was fortunate enough to be able to help provide some comfort and prayer to my fellow parishioners as a psychologist and theologian. But a feeling of helplessness still lingered within me. *Shouldn't I be doing more?* I wondered.

My mind went back to the overwhelming peace I felt as a boy when I would tread labyrinths on foot, calmly following the bending path in a way that made me feel at ease. An idea suddenly hit me: Perhaps our grieving church could benefit from labyrinths!

Others in the congregation shared my optimism, and together we imagined constructing a new labyrinth as a memorial to the three martyrs who died at our church. But though the group of us was hopeful, we were also concerned how others in the congregation might receive our idea. After all, many people believe that labyrinths—while technically sacred spaces dedicated to God—are an "alternate" spiritual tradition.

And so, I decided to write a liturgy. This, I hoped, would help convince people that labyrinths are indeed a useful tool for prayer, contemplation, and healing.

Of course, there was some skepticism at first. But as time passed and people found themselves lost in prayer and meditation, it quickly became clear that labyrinths had become a powerful source of spiritual therapy for the parishioners at Saint Stephen's—and especially for *me*.

Writing this liturgy ultimately made me realize that many people have no idea how to use a labyrinth. This book is designed to remedy that issue, providing a malleable guide and structure for how you can journey through the labyrinth and strengthen your relationship with God. I hope you will find a deeper sense of peace as you start your walk.

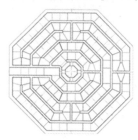

Figure 1. Labyrinth at Saint Stephen's Episcopal Church, Vestavia Hills, Alabama, USA

CHAPTER 1

A BRIEF INTRODUCTION TO LABYRINTHS

For too many people, the only time they have heard of a labyrinth is from the famous story from Greek mythology: the Labyrinth and the Minotaur. That labyrinth in Crete was where the intrepid explorer Theseus tracked down and killed the murderous Minotaur, a terrifying monster that was half-human and half-bull, who lived in it.

Figure 2. Drawing of the Mosaic in Villa Kerylos Beaulieu-sur-Mer Cap Ferrat, France. Finoskov, CC BY-SA 3.0 <https://creativecommons.org /licenses/by-sa/3.0>, via Wikimedia Commons. No changes were made.

To the Greeks, Theseus represents the traveler guided by divine instinct—represented in his case by a golden thread that he could follow—through the labyrinth of life to overcome the debased, animalistic side of his own nature. In many ways, that is still an important point of a labyrinth, as we seek union with God and strive to forsake our sinful ways.

Figure 3. Drawing of the Labyrinth at Chartres Cathedral, Chartres, France. Thurmanukyalur, CC BY-SA 3.0 <https://creativecommons.org/licenses /by-sa/3.0>, via Wikimedia Commons. No changes were made.

Figure 4. Labyrinth from the ceiling of the Ducal Palace in Mantua, Italy
(credit: tostphoto, iStock.com)

Labyrinths have been with humanity for millennia and were used for numerous religious purposes. The maze or labyrinth has appeared in the symbolism of ancient Egypt, nearly all early Mediterranean civilizations, and Indian and Tibetan cultures long before medieval Christianity subsumed it. In fact, thousands of years ago, at Nasca in Peru, people danced on labyrinths shaped like flowers and birds.

Most cultures share a symbolic understanding of labyrinths and mazes as places for expressing ideas of inner journeys through the confusing and conflicting pathways of the mind. The goals are often different, depending on whether the labyrinth is terminal or continuous, but that requires a little bit of explanation and some definitions.

Figure 5. Continuous labyrinth in Nasca desert of southern Peru. Diego Delso, CC BY-SA 4.0 <https://creativecommons.org/licenses/by-sa/4.0>, via Wikimedia Commons

Unfortunately, a maze and a labyrinth represent the same thing to the average person. In the Cretan story of the Minotaur, the labyrinth was a maze of doom: a particular type of labyrinth called *multicursal*, as there were numerous courses that dead-ended and in which travelers could be disoriented and possibly killed by the Minotaur. The multicursal labyrinth is therefore labeled more correctly in common usage as a maze, whereas a labyrinth has a single pathway—known as *unicursal*—in many courses. This unicursal labyrinth represents a journey within which the destination is clear. Yale musicologist and historian Craig M. Wright[1], who explored the archaeology of mazes, states that in the ancient world, the unicursal maze was the archetype for reality, although the multicursal maze seems to have been the literary and poetic ideal.

---

1. Wright, C.M. (2001). *The Maze and the Warrior: Symbols in architecture, theology, and music.* Harvard University Press.

The differentiation of these two terms—of maze and labyrinth—is important to define for our needs here. The Oxford Dictionary relays the following:

> maze /*māz*/ noun: a network of paths and hedges designed as a puzzle through which one has to find a way. "the house has a maze and a walled Italian garden"

> lab·y·rinth /ˈlab(ə)ˌrinTH/ noun: a complicated irregular network of passages or paths in which it is difficult to find one's way; a maze. "a labyrinth of passages and secret chambers"

Technically, there is no difference between these two terms unless we specify each of its purposes. In antiquity, mazes and labyrinths were the same thing; the difference was whether they were *in bono* or *in malo* (for good or for harm). To say that the ancients were wrong in naming their creations as labyrinths instead of mazes is the height of modern arrogance. The Oxford definition of maze might even remind us that we are looking for our way through the labyrinth in search of God, peace, or something else.

Most labyrinths were labeled as *labyrinthos termatikó* in Greek or *labyrinthum termina* in Latin. These labyrinths had a single path (set of courses) that started at the outside rim, winding inward, and ended in the center. A *labyrinthum iugis* or *labyrinthum contunua*[2] does not end in the center, but rather uses the center point as a position of worship or discovery from which the traveler must continue the symbolic journey, as if bringing the newfound treasure, usually peace or knowledge, back to the world by a slightly different route. These continuous labyrinths are therefore more theologically appropriate to Christian theology, as we are changed after any encounter with God and our paths continue, hopefully bringing the Gospel back to the world.

---

2. The Greek term *labyrinthum synechízontas* is almost never used.

Figure 6. Photo of continuous labyrinth at Trinity Episcopal Church, Abbeville, SC, USA.

Labyrinths and mazes are described by their overall shape—round, square, rectangular, octagonal, etc.—and number of courses—folded paths counted from the center to the edge. The Ducal Palace at Mantua is a rectangular six-course labyrinth, while Chartres is a round twelve-course labyrinth. The Chartres labyrinth has a *sacred geometry*, as it balances a sacred number of courses between the four cardinal points as on a cross.

Continuous labyrinth
RSPC 2019

Figure 7. Example plan of a *labyrinthum iugis* or *labyrinthum contunua (continuous labyrinth). Sketch provided by author.*

The Christian Purpose of Labyrinths

Modern scholars often state that the labyrinth was developed as a substitute for pilgrimage, but this is not necessarily so. The first recorded pilgrimage was that of Egeria, also called Etheria,[3] who journeyed sometime in the late fourth century.[4] Egeria was a nun who wanted to feel and see the land where Jesus had lived and walked, so made her journey there. She lived in the Holy Land for a few years, and she wrote about the local church practices and liturgies. Focusing on the journey and place helped her to feel more of a connection with her Lord, inspiring many other travelers to journey, either to the Holy Land or on other spiritual pilgrimages.

The earliest known Christian labyrinth was a church floor in St. Reparatus Church in El Asnam, Algeria, dating from 324 AD, the same year Constantine began to build St. Peter's in Rome.[5] This was before pilgrimages to the Holy Land or other sacred sites were common for Christians. In this labyrinth four separate five-course sections combine in quadrants to seek the center point, at which a verbal maze includes the words *SANTA ECLESIA* in several positions. These words, meaning "Holy Church" in Latin, are an important consideration for anyone thinking of undertaking a labyrinth journey. After all, the Church should be at the center of our wanderings and musings as we face towards God.

The labyrinth, like prayer itself, should be an inward effort (*labor intus*), west to east, from the lands of death to the new life and new light of both the rising sun and Rising Son, Jesus. Yet, Augustine said that worship that is passive and does not elicit a response or action is not fully worship. He has been paraphrased as saying: "If there be praise (or confession, petition, or response) and

---

3. A translation of her journey can be read at https://www.ccel.org/m/mcclure/etheria/etheria.htm
4. As indicated by references to contemporary materials: See https://www.dbu.edu/mitchell/ancient-christian-resources/egeria.html
5. Wright (2001), p. 16.

it is not of (or to) God, then it is not worship."[6] Action provides an aspect of dialogue with God that might be left out in purely passive ideas of praise.

According to some writers, Christianity first saw the maze as a symbol of the path of ignorance leading away from God. While little was written about labyrinths in the Christian tradition that we know of, by the fourteenth century labyrinths had recovered their positive symbolism and had come to denote the true way of belief[7]. In a strange idiosyncrasy of church history, until the eighteenth century, many cathedrals and churches had labyrinths as ways for people to substitute their walks for great pilgrimages to the Holy Land. Some speculate on the reasons that the labyrinths were removed or covered over, but none of the ideas seem to make complete sense[8].

Eventually, labyrinths became widely used in gardens and architecture, and beyond famous examples like the floor of Chartres Cathedral and the ceiling of the Ducal Palace in Mantua. Today, many wonderful examples remain with us around the world.

Mazes, as opposed to labyrinths (using the modern definitions), are not typically considered appropriate for centering, meditative prayer, as prayer is finding one's way out of difficulty, not risking getting trapped inside. Walking a labyrinth is a way of helping a person to center their prayers on God, contemplating the mysteries of our faith so that we can accept them and live with the more difficult aspects. This process is part of what we call contemplative prayer[9].

Though it might sound strange, many people do not know how to pray, or are kinesthetic learners who need to be doing something to help distract themselves so that they can focus on—and not

6. Furr, G.A., & Price, M. (1998). *The Dialog of Worship: Creating Space for Revelation and Response.* Smith & Helwys Publishing, p. 87.

7. Fontana D. (2001). *The secret language of symbols: a visual key to symbols and their meanings.* San Francisco: Chronicle Books.

8. C.f., Candolini, G. (2003). *Labyrinths: Walking toward the center.* Crossroad Publishing.

9. Danaher J. P. (2011). Contemplative prayer : a theology for the twenty-first century. Cascade Books.

be distracted away from—God. In the classic work on centering prayer, M. Basil Pennington[10] refers to the words of Paul in 1 Corinthians 2, which is worth reproducing here in its entirety:

[1]And I, brethren, when I came to you, came not with excellency of speech or of wisdom, declaring unto you the testimony of God. [2]For I determined not to know any thing among you, save Jesus Christ, and him crucified. [3]And I was with you in weakness, and in fear, and in much trembling. [4]And my speech and my preaching was not with enticing words of man's wisdom, but in demonstration of the Spirit and of power: [5]That your faith should not stand in the wisdom of men, but in the power of God.

[6]Howbeit we speak wisdom among them that are perfect: yet not the wisdom of this world, nor of the princes of this world, that come to nought: [7]But we speak the wisdom of God in a mystery, even the hidden wisdom, which God ordained before the world unto our glory: [8]Which none of the princes of this world knew: for had they known it, they would not have crucified the Lord of glory.

[9]But as it is written, Eye hath not seen, nor ear heard, neither have entered into the heart of man, the things which God hath prepared for them that love Him.

[10]But God hath revealed them unto us by His Spirit: for the Spirit searcheth all things, yea, the deep things of God. [11]For what man knoweth the things of a man, save the spirit of man which is in him? even so the things of God knoweth no man, but the Spirit of God. [12]Now we have received, not the spirit of the world, but the spirit which is of God; that we might know the things that are freely given to us of God. [13]Which things also we speak, not in the words which man's wisdom teacheth, but which the Holy Ghost teacheth; comparing spiritual things with spiritual.

[14]But the natural man receiveth not the things of the Spirit of God: for they are foolishness unto him: neither can

---

10. Pennington, M.B. (1982). *Centering Prayer: Renewing an ancient Christian prayer form.* Doubleday.

he know them, because they are spiritually discerned. [15]But he that is spiritual judgeth all things, yet he himself is judged of no man. [16]For who hath known the mind of the Lord, that he may instruct him? But we have the mind of Christ.

As Paul, most of us do not come to prayer in excellency of words or understanding, but in hope and faith. Often our understanding of faith is more akin to the father of the sick child in Mark 9:

[23]Jesus said unto him, If thou canst believe, all things are possible to him that believeth. [24]And straightway the father of the child cried out, and said with tears, Lord, I believe; help thou mine unbelief.

It is because of our unbelief that we need to pray and to focus our prayers on God, centering ourselves to seek God more fully. Too often, the idea of centering prayer is not on God, and not even on the self, but on a method or way of centering that becomes the object of the center itself[11]. Teresa of Avila taught that when we pray, especially without understanding of great words, we should consider ourselves as a castle, with God dwelling at the center of the soul, and desirous of each of us coming back to that center.[12]

Thomas Keating, a twentieth-century monk who is given a lot of the credit for reviving the Christian tradition of walking the labyrinth, focused on the idea of centering prayer as a form of contemplation. He discusses that the word "contemplation" used to mean different things. When you think of it, you probably see contemplation as being an intention of a future act. In the 1590s it meant reflecting on, studying, or meditating. But in the early Church it meant observation (*con-* means *with*; *templum* means an area for taking auguries, not just a place of worship[13]).

---

11. Pennington, M.B. (1985). Centering Prayer. In T. Keating, M.B. Pennington, and T.E. Clark (Eds). *Finding Grace at the Center*. Petersham, MA: St. Bede's Publications.

12. Kavanaugh, K. (2003). Contemplation and the stream of consciousness. In K.J. Egan (Ed.), *Carmelite Prayer: A tradition for the 21st century*. New York: Paulist Press.

13. https://www.etymonline.com/word/contemplate

In the early church, contemplative prayer was seen as a great thing, whereas from the sixth century on, Keating tells us that most people thought contemplative prayer indulgent. We know that recitation of scripture was seen as more important in many ways, especially following Erasmus's call: "I would to God that the plowman would sing a text of the Scripture at his plow and that the weaver would hum them to the tune of his shuttle."[14] Prayer was often considered to be essential for life, but only for focused purposes of worship and request. Keating says[15] that we should be praying for wisdom and an ever-increasing intimacy with God as *abba*, which is even more intimate than the word *father*. The problem is often that so many earthly fathers are not great examples of what a father should be, so people react against this term, analogizing our perfect Heavenly Father with our fallen, human ones.

What Keating was talking about can be transliterated from the Rule of Saint Benedict as: "Listen with the ear of your heart."[16] If we are to listen to God while praying, not just telling God what we want or think we need, then we must be in a spiritual and psychological condition to hear what God might be telling us. As the old adage goes, no prayer goes unanswered, but sometimes the answer is "no." Some authors, like Phileena Heurtz[17], remind us that to center ourselves in prayer, we also need to rest and make time for the centering. She recommends twenty minutes as a good average.

If one were to ask: "How does a labyrinth help our church," there are several answers given[18]. Improve mission, share worship, build community, and grow in wisdom are given as ways labyrinths help us.

14. Wallraff M., Seidel Menchi, S. & von Greyerz, K. (2016). *Basel 1516: Erasmus' edition of the New Testament.* Mohr Siebeck.

15. Keating, T. (1978). Contemplative prayer in Christian tradition. In T. Keating, M.B. Pennington, and T.E. Clark (Eds). *Finding Grace at the Center.* Petersham, MA: St. Bede's Publications.

16. Rule of Benedict, (prologue 1) accessed at: https://ccel.org/ccel/benedict/rule/rule.ii.html

17. Heuertz, P. (2010). *Pilgrimage of a soul: contemplative spirituality for the active life.* IVP Books.

18. Welch, S. (2010). *Walking the labyrinth: a spiritual and practical guide.* Canterbury Press.

Like prayer, however, labyrinths are best accomplished if we prepare ourselves beforehand and consider what we have done afterwards, listening for that small, soft voice of God within ourselves. In a lovely book on contemplative prayer, Christine Paintner and Lucy Wynkoop[19], both Benedictine sisters, remind us that preparing for truly listening for God's Word involves several steps. First, we must be reading God's Word (*lectio*), reflecting on God's Word (*meditatio*), responding to God's Word (*oratio*), resting with God's Word (*contemplatio*), and becoming God's Word (*operatio*). This is a set of operations that come into play while you journey through the labyrinth. Read and pray before walking, but make sure to continue this work while walking and afterwards.

Christian labyrinths should always be a reminder that God wants us to repent of our sins, but also to worship directly in a personal relationship of love and respect. One of the least-often cited bits of scripture that points to this level of love, respect, and hope is from Hosea 2:14-16, 19-20:

> [14]Therefore, I will now allure her,
>   and bring her into the wilderness,
>   and speak tenderly to her.
> [15]From there I will give her her vineyards,
>   and make the Valley of Achor a door of hope.
> There she shall respond as in the days of her youth,
>   as at the time when she came out of the land of Egypt.
> [16]On that day, says the Lord, you will call me, "My husband," and no longer will you call me, "My Baal." [17]For I will remove the names of the Baals from her mouth, and they shall be mentioned by name no more. [18]I will make for you a covenant on that day with the wild animals, the birds of the air, and the creeping things of the ground; and I will abolish the bow, the sword, and war from the land; and I will make you lie down in safety. [19]And I will take you for my wife forever; I will take you

---

19. Paintner, C. V. & Wynkoop, L. (2008). *Lectio divina: contemplative awakening and awareness.* Paulist Press.

for my wife in righteousness and in justice, in steadfast love, and in mercy. [20]I will take you for my wife in faithfulness; and you shall know the Lord.

Our relationship must change, and our closeness to God must remove us from our closeness to the world from which we came. In verse 16 above, most of us read the word "Baal" and think of a false god of the Canaanites. Here, however, it is used as a term that means "Master" or "Lord" to show that the relationship is different and hierarchical instead of loving and personal. This continues in the next verse in which the names of the Baals are the names of other masters or lords who held sway over God's people. These statements indicate a change in relationship of love and devotion that goes two ways, like in a marriage—instead of "Master," one becomes "Beloved."

The centering on God as Father in a pure, holy way will occasionally be uncomfortable, just as walking a labyrinth is sometimes uncomfortable or discomforting. It is, as Eugene Peterson[20] describes, a quest for a "middle voice."

> Prayer and spirituality feature participation, the complex participation of God and the human, His will and our wills. We do not abandon ourselves to the stream of grace and drown in the ocean of love, losing identity. We do not pull the strings that activate God's operations in our lives, subjecting God to our assertive identity. We neither manipulate God (active voice-0 nor are manipulated by God (passive voice). We are involved in the action and participate in its results but do not control or define it (middle voice). Prayer takes place in the middle voice. (p. 104)

For many of us, the theology of the labyrinths is to be understood as one of two things. First, with a *labyrinthos termatikó/labyrinthum termina,* such as the famous labyrinth at Chartres, we journey with Christ to Jerusalem as the center, pray, and then return the exact

---

20. Peterson, E. H. (1993). The contemplative pastor: returning to the art of spiritual direction. Wm. B. Eerdmans Pub.

way we came, or we simply walk off the labyrinth any way we like (because there are too many tourists on it at Chartres to walk back the way we came). This is less desirous theologically, as it either tells us to depart following any movement, not necessarily that of the Spirit, or to retrace our footsteps and end in the same place we began, which is far from the examples of the early disciples and saints.

A *labyrinthum iugis* or *labyrinthum contunua* is closer to the Christian ideal in many ways, as we never end up where we started, having been changed by the power of the Holy Spirit. After the resurrection, none of the disciples simply went home and carried on their lives as they were, nor should we after an encounter with God in a labyrinth. As Marshall McLuhan is famous for saying, "the Medium is the Message."[21] How we frame things and how we present them are the driving forces behind what labyrinth walkers take away from the experience. If we put forward a labyrinth that leaves ambiguity in its completion, we leave ambiguity as the final message of the labyrinth and the centering on God that applies in our lives.

---

21. McLuhan, M. (1964). *Understanding media: the extensions of man (6th printing)*. McGraw-Hill.

Before Walking the Labyrinth

Remember that walking the labyrinth is like going on pilgrimage. You need to prepare, even if briefly. While in the labyrinth, we need to be able to focus. Finally, we need to prayerfully and carefully consider our journey. Before, during, and after the experience is when we grow and learn. Therefore, each "walk" in this book begins with a preparation sequence of prayers or meditations on scripture, then the walk itself.

Before we embark on specific prayer circuits for seasons or days of the Church Year, it is important to stop and give suggestions for simply walking the labyrinth by yourself. You will discover many things about yourself and your relationship with God while walking the courses of a labyrinth. Some people find aspects of themselves they never knew about. Some develop patience and a willingness to do something that might seem awkward at first. Some people hear the small, soft voice of God when they slow down enough and open their hearts.

If you don't have access to a physical labyrinth built into a floor or yard, one can be painted onto canvas or concrete. Even if you need to drive a stake into the ground, tie on a piece of string, and use spray paint or chalk to mark out a labyrinth, that is just fine! Creating a labyrinth of your own that is easily accessible and can be used in quiet contemplation and peace is key. I have even used numerous children's toys lined up to mark off a labyrinth in a Sunday school classroom when that was all I had available.

Now, some may ask about the physical limitations of space that do not allow for a labyrinth to walk at all. If there is a public park near you, create your own by designating landmarks as places to turn and walk. Choose spots and make them a part of your own sacred geometry that helps you focus and get closer to God. Even if you are in a prison cell barely large enough to stand, you might be able to find movements that help you create a labyrinth and a way of praying.

In my office I have a block of wood that I sanded down and glued cardboard to in the form of a labyrinth. I can follow this with my finger and be spiritually on a labyrinth, losing myself into God's presence.

Maria Montessori used a similar sandpaper block technique to teach letters, and it is a wonderful thing to have the cardboard, sandpaper, fur, or other texture to rub your finger on to imagine walking the labyrinth.

Before you start walking (or rolling or however you are making it through), try to say a prayer. It might only be "Lord, help me to pray." It might be something more like:

> O Lord God, who laid the foundations of the earth and set the stars in their courses, guide me in Your Way. Help me to seek you out and find you so that I know you and know that you are God.

Much of the work of labyrinths is developing memory of muscle, of thought, and of spirit. As you proceed, pick a word or short verse to repeat, or if it is more comfortable, go through a list of what you have to be thankful for or what you repent of or need help with. Remember that you are trying to center yourself on God, releasing your burdens and stopping the focus only on yourself.

Although the Bible is full of many amazing verses and promptings for just this type of prayer, here are some suggestions for words and phrases to say while walking a labyrinth:

Words:		
Jesus	God	Love
Holy Spirit	Peace	Forgiveness

Short phrases:		
Give me Peace, O Lord	Forgive me	Show me your love
Heal me, O Christ	Hold me, Holy Spirit	Guide me
Help me, Lord	I seek you, Father	Lead me, Lord

Scripture	
Psalm 37:23-24:	"The Lord directs the steps of the godly. He delights in every detail of their lives. Though they stumble, they will never fall, for the Lord holds them by the hand."
Proverbs 16:9:	"We can make our plans, but the LORD determines our steps."
Psalm 23:1:	"The LORD is my shepherd; I shall not want."
Psalm 73:24:	"You guide me with your counsel, and afterward you will take me into glory."
Psalm 23:3:	"He restores my soul; He leads me in the paths of righteousness For His name's sake."
Matthew 6:33:	"But seek ye first the kingdom of God, and His righteousness; and all these things shall be added unto you."
Philippians 4:13:	"I can do all things through Christ which strengthen me."
Psalm 31:3:	"Since you are my rock and my fortress, for the sake of your name lead and guide me."
Psalm 16:11:	"You make known to me the path of life; you will fill me with joy in your presence, with eternal pleasures at your right hand."
Psalm 25:9:	"He guides the humble in what is right and teaches them His way."
Psalm 25:10:	"All the paths of the LORD are mercy and truth unto such as keep His covenant and His testimonies."
Psalm 37:23:	"The LORD makes firm the steps of the one who delights in Him;"
Jeremiah 10:23:	"LORD, I know that people's lives are not their own; it is not for them to direct their steps."
Psalm 43:3:	"O send out thy light and thy truth: let them lead me; let them bring me unto thy holy hill, and to thy tabernacles."

It is also good to develop your own prayer of thanksgiving for after the labyrinth. Such prayers can be as simple as "Amen" or much more complicated to include the growth and maturation of your relationship with God as that happens. My personal prayer afterwards tends to be:

> Thank you, Heavenly Father, for the ability to walk this labyrinth. Help me to focus on you and pray ceaselessly for others. Wash me through and let me bring your light into the world, blessing others as I go.

Find your own prayers, your own peace, your own relationship with God. Be blessed and be a blessing. When it is difficult, or when it is easy, focus on your relationship with God. Remember that you are always loved and never alone.

A Church Year of Labyrinth Walks

The Church Year is another way of gauging what is happening around us, just like the school year, fiscal year, or calendar year. For much of the Church, the year helps us to read through scripture and remember the most important parts of the Bible story in our lives. The labyrinth is an amazing way to help you to focus on these scriptural lessons in your life and your relationship with God.

Since the Church Year starts with Advent, the specific calendar of this book starts with Advent. However, you might be approaching this book at some other point in the calendar, or with some other need in your life. This reality is why the book begins with a labyrinth walk for what is called "Ordinary Time," which means any point in the Church Year that is not designated by a specific season or festival. The important part is that you pray to prepare, pray to walk, and pray to transition to your work in the world.

If weather prohibits the use of an outdoor labyrinth, a cloth one could be used indoors if available. If not on canvas or other cloth, a labyrinth can be marked off in tape on a floor, or even be outlined by chalk, rocks, toys, candles, etc. Park benches and trash cans could be markers for turning in a park if there were no other labyrinth to be your guide. Or, as there are labyrinths in this book, you can just follow along with your finger if need be. Don't let the lack of access to a physical outdoor or indoor labyrinth stop the use of these walks. Remember that they are developed to help focus on the possibilities of God, not the limitations of us mortals.

CHAPTER 2

ORDINARY TIME: THROUGHOUT THE CHURCH YEAR

This section contains two distinct forms of labyrinth journeys. The first is a deeply meditative guide to help you through any particular day of the year, focusing on you and your relationship with God. The other offers daily labyrinth walks for specific days of the week when you want to do a labyrinth walk but have less time or energy to focus fully on the fullness of that relationship. Both are useful in different times and days, depending on your needs and the environment around you.

A Labyrinth Walk for Any Day of the Year

This walk is appropriate for any time of the Church Year, but most especially for that called "Ordinary Time," when there is no special Feast Day. If desired and possible in the space, the color Green is preferred for decorations, banners, ribbons, etc.

This is the most general way of walking a labyrinth and is appropriate for any time of the year, whether there is a feast day or not.

Preparing before the Labyrinth

Sitting or standing, take a moment of quiet contemplation. Try to think of at least one thing to be grateful for, even if it is the ability to be alive in that space at that time. Read this from Isaiah 40:

> [3] A voice cries out: "In the wilderness prepare the way of the Lord, make straight in the desert a highway for our God. [4] Every valley shall be lifted up, and every mountain and hill be made low; the uneven ground shall become level, and the rough places a plain. Then the glory of the Lord shall be revealed, and all people shall see it together, for the mouth of the Lord has spoken."

A prayer before beginning the labyrinth:

> Oh Lord, my life has had ups and downs, curves and straight paths. Help me to lose myself in You, that I may find myself in You. Give me peace and clarity, O God, that I may be more content and joyful. Help me to love others and see You in all things, remembering that I am made in your image and worthy of your love.

For optional use, *when desired, a basin of Holy Water could be visited before entering the Labyrinth. Consider the following, dipping fingers into the water, then ritually washing the named parts:*

> Bless, O Lord, these hands, that they may provide care and
>   protection;
> Bless, O Lord, these eyes, that they may only see truth;

Bless, O Lord, these ears, that they may hear love;
Bless, O Lord, this mouth, that words of your glory are spoken;
Bless, O Lord, these feet, that they may walk in your way and
follow You always.

The Labyrinth

Begin the Labyrinth as is most expedient for you in that space. The Labyrinth courses may be followed in silence or in singing of a chant, such as "Ubi Caritas," or following one of the following options:

Option 1: *As you proceed through the labyrinth, pray for specific issues in your life that cause you concern or pain.*

When you get to a turn in the labyrinth courses, stop for a moment and pray something like: "Lord, turn me towards you and heal me of my worries."

When you approach the center of the labyrinth, stay in that center area and pray for those involved with all the issues which you have been thinking about during your journey.

Option 2: *Find a small stone or other easily carried object to represent your burdens. As you proceed through the labyrinth, pray about specific burdens and issues in your life that cause you concern or pain. See the stone or item you are carrying as representing those burdens.*

At each turn of the labyrinth, stop for a moment and seek out what losses you have had and add them symbolically to the stone.

When you get to the middle of the labyrinth, place the stone at God's feet. Pray for release from the yolk of those burdens and pains. Ask for a deeper relationship with God and with those whom you love. Pray for those who have caused you pain.

As you begin the journey out of the labyrinth, stop at each turn and focus on the blessings of friendship or learning that have resulted from all of your trials and tribulations. Prayerfully seek guidance for how to serve God better in loving friends, neighbors, and even enemies. Pray to know and understand how to serve and love yourself better and in keeping with God's will and scripture.

Option 3: *As you proceed through the labyrinth, read the following passages from scripture, and repeat as needed:*

"The Lord directs the steps of the godly. He delights in every detail of their lives. Though they stumble, they will never fall, for the Lord holds them by the hand."

"We can make our plans, but the Lord determines our steps."

"The LORD is my shepherd; I shall not want."

"You guide me with your counsel, and afterward You will take me into glory."

"He restores my soul; He leads me in the paths of righteousness For His name's sake."

"But seek ye first the kingdom of God, and His righteousness; and all these things shall be added unto you."

"Jesus spoke to the people once more and said, 'I am the light of the world. If you follow me, you won't have to walk in darkness, because you will have the light that leads to life.'"

"I can do all things through Christ which strengthen me."

"Since you are my rock and my fortress, for the sake of your name lead and guide me."

"You make known to me the path of life; you will fill me
with joy in your presence, with eternal pleasures at
your right hand."

"He guides the humble in what is right and teaches them
His way."

"All the paths of the LORD are mercy and truth unto
such as keep His covenant and His testimonies."

"LORD, I know that people's lives are not their own; it is
not for them to direct their steps."

"Seek the LORD and His strength, seek His face
continually."

"Trust in the LORD with all your heart And do not
lean on your own understanding. In all your ways
acknowledge Him, And He will make your paths
straight."

"O send out thy light and thy truth: let them lead me;
let them bring me unto thy holy hill, and to thy
tabernacles."

The Procession from Labyrinth into the World

*Prepare for going back to the world from your sacred space by saying this
prayer:*

Almighty and ever living God, I thank You for the centering of
my heart and mind on You, on your mercy, and on your love for
me and all of humanity. Please give me your mercy that my path
may be simple and wide, with no stumbling blocks before me.
Heal my brokenness where I am afflicted in mind, body, or spirit.
Strengthen me for your service, O God, that I may share with
others the peace and calm You have given to me. Have mercy on
all of us, beloved Lord, through Jesus Christ, with You and the
Holy Ghost, be all honor and glory, world without end. *Amen.*

Reflections from the Labyrinth

Today you were able to go through the labyrinth, whether physically or in your mind, completely or partially. Even if you did not immediately feel God's love, do not be discouraged! This practice will help you experience His presence in your life. Everyday labyrinth walks can foster and deepen your relationship with God and allow you to flourish spiritually. It is in reaching outward that we find inner peace.

Questions to ask yourself

- What were obstacles to your prayers on the labyrinth? Were there issues that you were dwelling on that intruded into your journey?

- As you journeyed through, did you start to become less self-conscious, or more? More self-aware, or less? Why might that be in either case?

- Were there moments that were difficult to focus on your prayer? Identifying them can help you to stop them from interfering.

- What new meaning can you find in the words of Psalm 9:1-2?

    > ¹I will give thanks to You, Lord, with all my heart; I will tell of all your wonderful deeds. ²I will be glad and rejoice in You; I will sing the praises of your name, O Most High.

- For whom did you pray? Yourself? Family? Friends? Enemies? The world?

Walking the Week: Sunday

If desired and possible in the space, the colors Violet or Royal Blue are preferred for decorations, banners, ribbons, etc.

Sunday is the Lord's Day and a day when we should be worshipping God together. For some this is not possible, for others it is not enough. For whatever reason, a journey on the Labyrinth is an excellent activity to continue your Sunday contemplations and praise.

Preparing before the Labyrinth

Sitting or standing, take a moment of quiet contemplation and then read the following scripture to reflect on God as you relate to God.

> Dear God, this day is dedicated to You. Help me to journey through this labyrinth and find your love. Through twists and turns, lead me to You. Let me seek and find peace, and leave behind hate, jealousy, or any other feelings and thoughts that keep me from You. Strengthen my heart, O God, to do as You commanded and love others as You love us.

The Labyrinth

Begin the Labyrinth as is most expedient for that space. The Labyrinth courses may be followed in silence, or you can pray aloud or sing a chant, such as "Jesus, I love you," or rounds of "Seek ye first the Kingdom of God" as appropriate to your traditions. At the center of the Labyrinth, contemplate the union of your soul with God. Praise God with personal worship.

The Procession from Labyrinth into the World

> Jesus, our savior and friend, this day reminds me that you both died for me and lived for me. Share with me your peace and mercy. Help me to love other people and overcome my fears and concerns that separate me from you. Help me to remember that all people are made in your image and that you love them, even when we don't act as we should. Give me mercy and the ability to be merciful, praising you always. *Amen.*

Reflections from the Labyrinth

In the early Church, believers came together to break bread and pray. They sometimes faced persecution, and sometimes did not worship well and were rebuked for losing focus. In the labyrinth, focus is key. Each Sunday should be a reminder of Easter and the resurrection of Jesus that overcomes death for us all.

Questions to ask yourself

- In the old language of the Church, we asked God to have mercy on us "miserable sinners," with miserable meaning in "need of mercy." What mercy are you in need of?

- When you journeyed the labyrinth, were you able to consider why we dedicate Sundays to God?

- How can you worship God more fully?

Walking the Week: Monday

If desired and possible in the space, the colors Violet or Royal Blue are preferred for decorations, banners, ribbons, etc.

Monday is the beginning of the work week and a day of dread for many. The labyrinth can be used to focus on the hope and possibilities of this new week, even if by the time you start the labyrinth Monday has already happened. Joy and love always win.

Preparing before the Labyrinth

Sitting or standing, take a moment of quiet contemplation and then read the following scripture from 1 Thessalonians 5:14-18:

> And we urge you, my siblings, to admonish the unruly, encourage the fainthearted, help the weak, and be patient with everyone. Make sure that no one repays evil for evil. Always pursue what is good for one another and for all people. Rejoice at all times. Pray without ceasing. Give thanks in every circumstance, for this is God's will for you in Christ Jesus.

The Labyrinth

Begin the Labyrinth as is most expedient for that space. The Labyrinth courses may be followed in silence or in praying "Lord, give me strength," "Lord Give me Hope," of "Lord give me patience" as appropriate to your life at that moment. At the center of the labyrinth, say a special prayer of hope, such as:

> Dear God, I bless You for this day. I am alive and have hope. Please make this week dedicated to your glory and peace. Help me share kindness and love with people. Give me humility to listen to others and not feel compelled to seek attention. Let me find myself in You. *Amen.*

The Procession from Labyrinth into the World

> O Creator of the universe and of time itself, thank You for the beginning of this week. Enable and empower me to help build

your kingdom and share your love with all people, even when I don't want to. Create a clean heart of charity within me that can care for others more than for myself. Let this week be a week of kindness and compassion. *Amen.*

Reflections from the Labyrinth

Monday is a reminder of the connectedness of life. We should be able to remember the goodness and mercy of all people, even when they are not being good or merciful. Each new week is an opportunity to serve God and bring healing to the world. Let God heal you and strengthen you to help you heal others.

Questions to ask yourself

- Are there new opportunities to serve God this week that you are excited for?
- How can you center yourself so that you are able to enjoy this coming week more fully and all that you have to do?
- If there are issues that cause you stress in this week, how can you leave them at the center of the labyrinth?

Walking the Week: Tuesday

If desired and possible in the space, the colors Violet or Royal Blue are preferred for decorations, banners, ribbons, etc.

Tuesday is a day of focus and energy for many people. Typically, among the most productive days of the week, a question to face is how you can become productive in your prayerfulness and faithfulness. Rather than walking a labyrinth simply for focus, try to walk the labyrinth for celebration that you are a beloved child of God and empowered to worship.

Preparing before the Labyrinth

Sitting or standing, take a moment of quiet contemplation and then read the following prayer to reflect on celebrating relationship with Christ:

> Jesus, our brother, comforter, redeemer, and friend. You took on human flesh and became one with us to better know and love us. You felt our joy and our pain. Bind me to you, Lord of All, so that I may see the reasons to celebrate and praise you. As I journey through this labyrinth, grant me strength and courage to see beyond myself so that I can celebrate you with other people in the Church Triumphant as well as the Church around me.

The Labyrinth

Begin the Labyrinth as is most expedient for that space. The Labyrinth courses may be followed in silence or with prayers of celebration. Try to focus on not only issues of productivity at work, but on the productivity of prayer and kindness. While you journey, perhaps try this prayer attributed to St. Francis:

> Lord, make us instruments of your peace. Where there is hatred, let us sow love; where there is injury, pardon; where there is discord, union; where there is doubt, faith; where there is despair, hope; where there is darkness, light; where there is sadness, joy. Grant that we may not so much seek to be consoled as to console; to be understood as to understand;

to be loved as to love. For it is in giving that we receive; it is in pardoning that we are pardoned; and it is in dying that we are born to eternal life. *Amen.*

—St. Francis of Assisi[1]

The Procession from Labyrinth into the World

Lover of my soul, who has granted me this day, thank You for this time to celebrate You and your Kingdom. Thank You for the ability to journey through this labyrinth and recognize the joys of life that I pass by unaware. Thank You for your life among us in all Three Persons, Father, Son, and Holy Spirit. *Amen.*

Reflections from the Labyrinth

Each Tuesday should be a continuation of our love and devotion, recognizing that the blessings God gives us always outweigh anything else we experience. It is an opportunity to renew and strengthen our relationship with God as the work week continues.

Questions to ask yourself

* What does productivity mean to you at this point in your life? How can you be more productive in serving God and other people?

* How can you avoid trying to serve mammon (money)? Where are your fears regarding money, and how can you pray for relief from those fears?

* Where do you find yourself to be most helpful to the Church?

---

1. Book of Common Prayer (1979), p. 833

Walking the Week: Wednesday

If desired and possible in the space, the colors Violet or Royal Blue are pre-ferred for decorations, banners, ribbons, etc.

Wednesday is often called "hump day" because it is the middle or "hump" of the work week over which we must pass in order to reach the weekend. On such a day, it is important to seek out how we can focus on God in all Three Persons of the Trinity instead of only looking forward to the weekend.

Preparing before the Labyrinth

Sitting or standing, take a moment of quiet contemplation and then read the following scripture to reflect on the message of the Trinity called the Great Commission from Matthew 28:

> [16] Then the eleven disciples went to Galilee, to the mountain where Jesus had told them to go. [17] When they saw him, they worshiped him; but some doubted. [18] Then Jesus came to them and said, "All authority in heaven and on earth has been given to me. [19] Therefore go and make disciples of all nations, baptizing them in the name of the Father and of the Son and of the Holy Spirit, [20] and teaching them to obey everything I have commanded you. And surely I am with you always, to the very end of the age."

Even the disciples had doubts, so it is okay if you do as well. Pray about this and consider the person in Mark 9 who admits that he does not fully understand belief, but wants to:

> [23] Jesus said to him, "If you can believe, all things *are* possible to him who believes." [24] Immediately the father of the child cried out and said with tears, "Lord, I believe; help my unbelief!"

The Labyrinth

Begin the Labyrinth as is most expedient for that space. The Labyrinth courses may be followed in silence or in repeating "Lord, Help my unbelief."

The Procession from Labyrinth into the World

O Lord, who forms the foundation of my belief, help me where I falter. Help my unbelief so that my faith is strong. Help me to see You in all things and cast aside my doubts and misunderstandings. Subdue my passions for all but You, O God, that I may love other people without fear and concern. Strengthen me to love and serve You better, Holy Trinity, Three in One, so that each day is lived in your honor and to your glory. *Amen.*

Reflections from the Labyrinth

Different faiths are everywhere and should not frighten us. Instead, they should help strengthen and enrich our own faith. After all, our world is built with many ways of understanding the Divine. And though we firmly believe that we are correct in knowing God as the Three Persons of Father, Son, and Holy Spirit, we should not let other people's faiths turn us to hatred or insecurity.

Questions to ask yourself

- How do you relate to God? How do you imagine God as being three Persons at the same time as being each distinct person?

- Do you see yourself in God? How does this help strengthen your faith instead of separating you from the love of God?

- Does Wednesday mean a glide towards the weekend more than a day to celebrate and strengthen your relationship with God?

Walking the Week: Thursday

If desired and possible in the space, the colors Violet or Royal Blue are preferred for decorations, banners, ribbons, etc.

Thursday is a time of anticipation for the working world since it signals that the weekend is nearing. It is also an opportunity to see the approach of the Sabbath and a time to reflect on the week.

Preparing before the Labyrinth

Sitting or standing, take a moment of quiet contemplation and then read the following scripture to reflect on hope:

> "For I know the plans I have for you," declares the Lord, "plans to prosper you and not to harm you, plans to give you hope and a future." *Jeremiah 29:11 NIV*

> Thou knowest my downsitting and mine uprising, thou understandest my thought afar off. Thou compassest my path and my lying down, and art acquainted with all my ways. For there is not a word in my tongue, but, lo, O Lord, thou knowest it altogether. *Psalm 139:2-4 KJV*

> Lord, you have helped me make it though this week, through trials and tribulations, things done and left undone, known and unknown. Bless me as I journey through this labyrinth. Let each turn and curve remind me to center myself on you and be grateful for all of your loving kindness.

The Labyrinth

Begin the Labyrinth as is most expedient for that space. The Labyrinth courses may be followed in silence or repeating, "Create a clean heart within me, O God, and strengthen me to your service."

The Procession from Labyrinth into the World

> Lord, let this week continue to be dedicated to You. Support all my work and prayers to be to your glory. Continue to me your

presence and protection with clarity of mind and openness of heart. *Amen.*

Reflections from the Labyrinth

Each day is a gift from God, a time that is blessed and full of potential. Each day is to be filled with worship of the God who loves us and gave us more than we could ever deserve. As the week continues, open yourself to the small, soft voice of God in all that you do. Find peace and happiness, even when it might seem there are none. Just as God knows every hair on your head, God knows what you are going through and sees beyond this moment.

Questions to ask yourself

- How does this day compare to others in your ability to focus on God while journeying the labyrinth? What made it different if it was?

- As you went through the labyrinth, were you able to let go of your concerns and embrace that God loves you and has a plan for you?

- Did your labyrinth journey help you look forward at what is to come, or look back at what has been? Why might that be?

Walking the Week: Friday

If desired and possible in the space, the colors Violet or Royal Blue are preferred for decorations, banners, ribbons, etc.

The end of the week is often a time of celebration and anticipated fun. Whether it is spent enjoying a dinner with friends, worship services, or relaxation, Fridays can look different for most people. With a labyrinth journey, the coming of the weekend is an opportunity to focus on God and renew and strengthen your relationship with Him.

Preparing before the Labyrinth

Sitting or standing, take a moment of quiet contemplation and then read the following scripture to reflect on coming rest:

Truly my soul finds rest in God; my salvation comes from Him. Truly he is my rock and my salvation; he is my fortress, I will never be shaken. *Psalm 62: 1-2 NIV*

Praise be to the Lord, who has given rest to His people Israel just as he promised. Not one word has failed of all the good promises He gave through his servant Moses. *1 Kings 8:56 NIV*

I will refresh the weary and satisfy the faint. *Jeremiah 31:25 NIV*

The Labyrinth

Begin the Labyrinth as is most expedient for that space. Repeating words of praise and thanksgiving or asking for peace at each turn of the labyrinth courses is advisable. If you have trouble thinking of specifics, please try something like this:

Thank You, Lord, for this day and this week.

The Procession from Labyrinth into the World

> On this sixth day, O Lord, You created so much and set the world in order. Let my world be put right, O God, that You are my focus, my rock, and my strength. Help me to turn always to You. Let this day be consecrated to loving You and other people more than focusing on loving myself. *Amen.*

Reflections from the Labyrinth

For early Christians, Friday evening was still considered the start of the weekly Sabbath. Celebrations and meals with family were among the norms until society began to veer away from this practice and focus on individual pleasure. In the labyrinth, there is an opportunity to turn back to God and find peace and rest in Him.

Questions to ask yourself

- How can pleasure be magnified by turning the focus towards God in our lives?

- Where are opportunities to free ourselves of the societal expectations for Friday nights and replace them with more loving and fulfilling service to God and each other?

- How does this day differ from any other day in your life? Was the journey through the labyrinth more or less difficult than the rest of the week? Why?

Walking the Week: Saturday

If desired and possible in the space, the colors Violet or Royal Blue are preferred for decorations, banners, ribbons, etc.

Saturday is the Jewish Sabbath, the day the Lord set aside so we can rest. Each Saturday should be a remembrance of the physical and spiritual restoration we can get because of Jesus.

Preparing before the Labyrinth

Sitting or standing, take a moment of quiet contemplation and then read the following from Isaiah 58:13-14 (NIV):

> "If you keep your feet from breaking the Sabbath
> and from doing as you please on my holy day,
> if you call the Sabbath a delight
> and the Lord's holy day honorable,
> and if you honor it by not going your own way
> and not doing as you please or speaking idle words,
> then you will find your joy in the Lord,
> and I will cause you to ride in triumph on the heights of
>   the land
> and to feast on the inheritance of your father Jacob."
> For the mouth of the Lord has spoken.

The Labyrinth

Begin the Labyrinth as is most expedient for that space. The Labyrinth courses may be followed in silence or repeating "God, give me rest" or "I find my rest in you."

The Procession from Labyrinth into the World

> "Come to me, all you who are weary and burdened, and I will give you rest. Take my yoke upon you and learn from me, for I am gentle and humble in heart, and you will find rest for your souls. For my yoke is easy and my burden is light." *Matthew 11:28-30 (NIV)*

Creator, sustainer, redeemer, you have given me this time to rest. Help me to use it to refresh myself that I might better serve You in humility and peace. Give me strength and the grace to let others serve me as well. Help me to be a better friend to all and show your image through my kindness. *Amen.*

Reflections from the Labyrinth

Saturday is a golden day of rest to much of the world. Even if you have work on a Saturday, rest might still be found by focusing on your relationship with God. Your soul should find rest, even if your body cannot.

Questions to ask yourself

- How can you rest when you still have obligations and duties required of you on a Saturday?
- Should there be another form of rest if you no longer work?
- What are we really doing on the sabbath to keep it holy, even if we are busier than during the week?

CHAPTER 3

ADVENT LABYRINTH WALKS

Advent literally means "to come" and is a time of anticipation and renewal as we prepare for Christmas. We anticipate the birth of Jesus and renew our faith and love of our God who gives us so much more than we can ever know. Advent is a four-week period beginning with the fourth Sunday before Christmas and continuing through Christmas Eve. It is of special significance that Advent is the beginning of the Church Year and sets the mood for the entire year as one of hope, peace, joy, and love.

Many people think of Advent as represented by the Advent Wreath—a circle of four candles, typically intertwined with holly or other greenery. Each of the four weeks are focused on the following order: The first week centers on Hope and is illuminated by the Prophecy Candle (purple). The second week is focused on Peace. It is symbolized by the Bethlehem Candle (also purple). The third week is celebrating Joy and is indicated by the Shepherd's Candle (pink). The fourth week concentrates on Love. The final candle, known as the Angel's Candle (purple), completes the wreath. Each of these should help you to focus your Labyrinth journeys so that you can be more authentically in the season.

If you have an advent wreath, it is a good idea to have it near your labyrinth so that your gaze occasionally falls upon the candles and the traditions of the season. The labyrinth can also be a wreath itself, surrounded by the four candles while you walk. Be creative and speak to your own imagination of how you get closer to God.

Advent 1: Walk of Hope

If desired and possible in the space, the colors Violet or Royal Blue are preferred for decorations, banners, ribbons, etc.

Though it is often dismissed as less important than others, the first week of Advent is a key to helping you build the anticipation for the most amazing and world-changing moment in history: When God became human. There is nothing that could give us more hope than the gift of Jesus, even if we already know the story and do not always understand what it means.

Preparing before the Labyrinth

Sitting or standing, take a moment of quiet contemplation and then read the following scripture to reflect on hope:

May the God of hope fill you with all joy and peace in believing, so that by the power of the Holy Spirit you may abound in hope. *Romans 15:13*

Now faith is the assurance of things hoped for, the conviction of things not seen. *Hebrews 11:1*

For in this hope we were saved. Now hope that is seen is not hope. For who hopes for what he sees? But if we hope for what we do not see, we wait for it with patience. *Romans 8:24–25*

Why, my soul, are you downcast? Why so disturbed within me? Put your hope in God, for I will yet praise Him, my Savior and my God. *Psalm 42:11*

But those who hope in the Lord will renew their strength. They will soar on wings like eagles; they will run and not grow weary, they will walk and not be faint. *Isaiah 40:31*

Either say or sing:

Our Father, who art in heaven,
 hallowed be thy Name,
 thy kingdom come,

thy will be done,
     on earth as it is in heaven.
Give us this day our daily bread.
And forgive us our trespasses,
     as we forgive those who trespass against us.
And lead us not into temptation,
     but deliver us from evil.
For thine is the kingdom, and the power, and the glory,
     for ever and ever. Amen.

The Labyrinth

Begin the Labyrinth as is most expedient for that space. The Labyrinth courses may be followed in silence or in singing a chant, such as The Light of Christ! Alleluia! or rounds of "Seek ye first the Kingdom of God."

Creator, sustainer, redeemer of all, I praise You and thank You for the ability to follow the wise who have traveled afar seeking You. Give me continual hope in your kingdom and hope for your people. Inspire in my heart the drive to continually seek You. Even when I cannot walk or roll through across the ground, empower me to follow wherever You lead, praising You and loving You now and always. *Amen.*

The Procession from Labyrinth into the World

Spirit of love and peace, who came to earth for our salvation, lead me on to your love. Show my heart and mind the promise of the true hope that binds me to You and to other people. Give me further hope to see your Kingdom on Earth as beautiful, just, and merciful as your Kingdom in Heaven. Tie all of us together with unbreakable cords of hope that we may build this Kingdom for You and with You. *Amen.*

Reflections from the Labyrinth

On this journey, you pilgrimaged through many places that may not be filled with peace, but you were never alone. God was there to give you hope. Hope is a cord that binds the past and present to the future. Hope endures while we draw breath and only ends when we have seen the fruition of that hope. If you were able to pray during the labyrinth, reflect on the hopes that you have, and evaluate if these hopes were expressed in your prayers. If you were not able to pray, what hopes or fears kept you from being able to pray?

Questions to ask yourself

- When you journeyed the labyrinth, were you able to form words or images around your hopes? If you did, could you write them down, or are they too fleeting and difficult to express in words?

- What do you truly hope for? Is your greatest hope similar to your greatest fear?

- Where does hope come from? Is it from your heart, or is it a gift that God places in your heart?

- Why does not seeing our hopes come to fruition so often damage our faith?

- Why during Advent do we have a week dedicated to Hope? Where is hope fulfilled in scripture?

- Since Jesus has already been here and the Holy Spirit is still with us, what are we really hoping for?

Advent 2: Walk of Peace

If desired and possible in the space, the colors Violet or Royal Blue are preferred for decorations, banners, ribbons, etc.

This week is the week where we contemplate what peace really is and what it should look like in our lives. Peace does not mean quiet. Peace does not always mean calm. Peace will mean different things to you at different moments of your life, and that is one focus for these journeys on the labyrinth.

Preparing before the Labyrinth

Sitting or standing, take a moment of quiet contemplation and then read the following scripture to set your heart at peace:

> [26]But the Advocate, the Holy Spirit, whom the Father will send in my name, will teach you all things and will remind you of everything I have said to you. [27]Peace I leave with you; my peace I give you. I do not give to you as the world gives. Do not let your hearts be troubled and do not be afraid. [28]"You heard me say, 'I am going away and I am coming back to you.' If you loved me, you would be glad that I am going to the Father, for the Father is greater than I. *John 14:26–28 (NIV)*

Give me your peace, O God, and hear me when I call to You.
> I am troubled and fight others in ways that I do not
> always know.

Give me your peace, O God, and hear me when I call to You.
> I cause pain in myself and in others because I lack faith in
> You and your promises.

Give me your peace, O God, and hear me when I call to You.
> Send me angels of Peace, beloved Lord, that I can
> overcome my fear and be glad for other people.

Give me your peace, O God, and hear me when I call to You.
> Help me to return to You, Holy One, and let my heart no
> longer be troubled.

Give me your peace, O God, and hear me when I call to You.
> Let me not be afraid, but help me to trust in your peace.

The Labyrinth

Now begin the Labyrinth as is most expedient for you in that space. The Labyrinth courses may be followed in silence or in repeating the word "Peace" or phrase "Give us your peace" while walking. When you have completed the Journey, stand or be seated in silent prayer until you feel ready to move on with closing prayers.

The Procession from Labyrinth into the World

"Come unto me, all ye that labor and are heavy laden, and I will give you rest. Take my yoke upon you, and learn of me; for I am meek and lowly in heart: and ye shall find rest unto your souls. For my yoke is easy, and my burden is light." *(Matthew 11:28-30)*

O God of Peace, lover of concord, who sent your Son to be the Prince of Peace, plant faith and true peace in my heart this day, so that I may abandon fear and doubt. Let all wars and divisions cease. Take away the hatred and jealousy that destroy the unity of your people. Amen.

Peace I leave with you, my peace I give unto you: not as the world giveth, give I unto you. Let not your heart be troubled, neither let it be afraid. The Lord of Peace, who sent Angels with messages of Peace, enfold us in tranquility and happiness. And the blessing of God Almighty, the Father, the Son, and the Holy Ghost, be amongst us, and remain with us always. *Amen.*

John 14:27

Reflections from the Labyrinth

This was a pilgrimage of peace, accompanied by the Holy Spirit. Peace is a state in which we find a center of calm because our faith in God is strong. As you travel through the labyrinth seeking peace, focus within your heart and pray that peace begins there and translates out to the world through you. We often pray for peace in the world, but rarely start with peace within our own hearts.

Questions to ask yourself

- What does peace really look like in your everyday life?

- What are the sources of discord in your relationships?

- Are there times when you are the one destroying your own peace? Why might that be?

- Is personal peace enough, or does peace require others to be peaceful?

- Why during Advent do we have a week dedicated to Peace? Have you considered this as you read the biblical accounts of Jesus' birth?

- Why was Jesus necessary to help real peace enter the world? What does it mean that there is still war after Jesus came?

Advent 3: Walk of Joy

If desired and possible in the space, the colors Violet or Royal Blue are preferred for decorations, banners, ribbons, etc.

The week of Joy is the week when we should be focusing on what is joy, what brings us joy, and how joy is expressed in our lives. Happiness is an outward expression, whereas joy is an internal feeling of internal selfless contentment and peace, even through trials and tribulations.

Preparing before the Labyrinth

Sitting or standing, take a moment of quiet contemplation and then read the following scripture passages:

> And, lo, the angel of the Lord came upon them, and the glory of the Lord shone round about them: and they were sore afraid. And the angel said unto them, Fear not: for, behold, I bring you good tidings of great joy, which shall be to all people. For unto you is born this day in the city of David a Saviour, which is Christ the Lord. *Luke 2:9-11*

> When they had heard the king, they departed; and, lo, the star, which they saw in the east, went before them, till it came and stood over where the young child was. When they saw the star, they rejoiced with exceeding great joy. And when they were come into the house, they saw the young child with Mary his mother, and fell down, and worshipped him: and when they had opened their treasures, they presented unto him gifts; gold, and frankincense and myrrh. *Matthew 2:9-11*

The Labyrinth

Begin the Labyrinth as is most expedient for you in that space. The Labyrinth courses may be followed in silence or in repeating the word "Joy" or phrase, "Give us your peace" while walking. It is entirely appropriate, if desired, to listen to "Jesu, Joy of Man's Desire" or other joyful Advent music while you walk the labyrinth. Alternatively, read these prayers before your journey:

Let them shout for joy, and be glad, that favour my righteous cause: yea, let them say continually, Let the Lord be magnified, which hath pleasure in the prosperity of His servant. *Psalm 35:27*

But let all those that put their trust in thee rejoice: let them ever shout for joy, because thou defendest them: let them also that love thy name be joyful in thee. *Psalm 5:11*

For His anger endureth but a moment; in His favour is life: weeping may endure for a night, but joy cometh in the morning. *Psalm 30:5*

Let the saints be joyful in glory: let them sing aloud upon their beds. *Psalm 149:5*

He maketh the barren woman to keep house, and to be a joyful mother of children. Praise ye the Lord. *Psalm 113:9*

Make me to hear joy and gladness; that the bones which thou hast broken may rejoice. *Psalm 51:8*

Go your way, eat the fat, and drink the sweet, and send portions unto them for whom nothing is prepared: for this day is holy unto our Lord: neither be ye sorry; for the joy of the Lord is your strength. *Nehemiah 8:10*

And I will rejoice in Jerusalem, and joy in my people: and the voice of weeping shall be no more heard in her, nor the voice of crying. Isaiah 65:19

Then shall the virgin rejoice in the dance, both young men and old together: for I will turn their mourning into joy, and will comfort them, and make them rejoice from their sorrow. *Jeremiah 31:13*

Yet I will rejoice in the Lord, I will joy in the God of my salvation. *Habakkuk 3:18*

And David spake to the chief of the Levites to appoint their brethren to be the singers with instruments of musick, psalteries and harps and cymbals, sounding, by lifting up the voice with joy. *1 Chronicles 15:16*

> But the fruit of the Spirit is love, joy, peace, longsuffering, gentleness, goodness, faith, meekness, temperance: against such there is no law. *Galatians 5:22-23*

> Blessed are ye, when men shall hate you, and when they shall separate you from their company, and shall reproach you, and cast out your name as evil, for the Son of man's sake. Rejoice ye in that day, and leap for joy: for, behold, your reward is great in heaven: for in the like manner did their fathers unto the prophets. *Luke 6:22-23*

The Procession from Labyrinth into the World

A reading from Luke 15:10

Jesus said "I say unto you, that likewise joy shall be in heaven over one sinner that repenteth, more than over ninety and nine just persons, which need no repentance" (*Luke 15:7*).

Help me to be filled with joy and repentance so that I will come to share with all the saints and angels in your heavenly kingdom. O God of Joy, who told us that there is exceeding joy in the presence of the angels of God over one sinner who repents, fill me with the joy of this advent season. Prepare my heart as a cradle for You, our King and Lord. Remind me that it is not through the material that I am filled, but by every word from you. *Amen.*

Reflections from the Labyrinth

This was a pilgrimage of joy through foreign lands often covered by conquest and sorrow. Joy is often confused with happiness, a fleeting feeling of pleasure that is derived from things outside of you. Joy is about the soul. It is the elation you feel deep in your spirit because of

God. Joy is a long-term state of being, not simply a single, transient moment of pleasure.

Questions to ask yourself

- Why during Advent do we have a week dedicated to Joy?
- When have you felt real joy in your life? When have you felt some happiness, but not the elation that defines joy?
- Why can we be joyful, even in the midst of sorrow?
- Why is it easy to crush happiness, but joy is not easily overcome?
- Why do we describe Jesus' birth as bringing joy to the world?

Advent 4: Walk of Love

If desired and possible in the space, the colors Violet or Royal Blue are preferred for decorations, banners, ribbons, etc.

In this week of journeys through the labyrinth, we should be focusing on what love means to us. What does the love of God really mean to us, especially if we use the word so much it has lost its meaning? What is love really if our experiences of love are broken and focused on control instead of perfect freedom? There is a great joy in focusing on the simplest of pure theologies: Jesus loves me, this I know…

Preparing before the Labyrinth

Sitting or standing, take a moment of quiet contemplation and then read the following scripture readings:

> Greater love has no one than this: to lay down one's life for one's friends. *John 15:13*

> One of the teachers of the law came and heard them debating. Noticing that Jesus had given them a good answer, he asked him, "Of all the commandments, which is the most important?" "The most important one," answered Jesus, "is this: 'Hear, O Israel: The Lord our God, the Lord is one. Love the Lord your God with all your heart and with all your soul and with all your mind and with all your strength.' The second is this: 'Love your neighbor as yourself.' There is no commandment greater than these."

> "Well said, teacher," the man replied. "You are right in saying that God is one and there is no other but Him. To love Him with all your heart, with all your understanding and with all your strength, and to love your neighbor as yourself is more important than all burnt offerings and sacrifices."

> When Jesus saw that he had answered wisely, he said to him, "You are not far from the kingdom of God." And from then on no one dared ask him any more questions. *Mark 12: 28-34*

Guide my steps, O Lord, Help me to come to that Holy Hill of your presence within my heart. Let each course of this labyrinth remove me from the pain and suffering that keeps me from fulfilling your commandment to love one another as You love us. Help me to love others as I learn to love You.

The Labyrinth

Begin the Labyrinth as is most expedient for that space. The Labyrinth courses may be followed in silence or in repeating the word "Love" or phrase "Give us your love" while walking. You may also consider singing a hymn, such as "What wondrous love is this, O my soul."

The Procession from Labyrinth into the World

Enfold me in the wings of your love, O God. Help my feet and heart to lead me to You. Strengthen my love for others so that I can love myself and my enemies as much as my friends, knowing that we are all your children and made in your image. Encourage and enable me to see the miracle of the nativity and the boundless love for all the world that Jesus' birth represents. Help me to bring that love to everyone, ever in your Holy Name I pray. *Amen.*

Reflections from the Labyrinth

A pilgrimage of Love is an easy walk for a difficult cause. Or, perhaps it is a difficult journey for an easy cause. Your life is different from any other ever lived. Part of the difficulty can be summed up by the question: Who do you *really* love? So often we hear the word love as if it is only romantic love. The Labyrinth is to get you to consider what and whom you love all around you, and what love really means. In scripture, there are many different words used for love, most common in the New Testament are *agape* and *eros*. *Agape* is love centered on selflessness, putting the other first. It is the true love of Christ and is almost perfectly oppositional to eros. *Eros* is an intense emotional and physical attraction that some define as love, as it may include devotion. *Ludus* is the playful love of children–accepting, friendly, and full of potential. *Storge* is most commonly thought of as the devoted love of parents for their children but is also a deeply committed friendship. *Pragma* is a practical or longstanding love for people, a deep commitment to others who might be neighbors or peripheral to our lives, but still important to us. *Philia* pertains to the deep camaraderie that is developed between brothers in arms who have fought side by side on the battlefield. It is about showing loyalty to your friends, sacrificing for them, and sharing your emotions with them. Finally, and probably least considered by many people, is *Philautia*, or love of the self. Considering all of these forms of love are essential parts of finding the Hope, Peace, and Joy that constitute the fullest forms of love. Only through loving God do we truly love each other and love ourselves well. People often remember that Jesus loved us enough to die for us, but sometimes forget that he loved us enough to live for us.

Questions to ask yourself

- Why during Advent do we have a week dedicated to Love? Have you considered this as you read the biblical accounts of Jesus' birth?

- What were the thoughts of love that you felt during the labyrinth? Had you opened yourself up to try and feel love?

- How can we bring love into our hearts if we are burning with rage or hate or fear?

- Can love exist without Hope, Peace, and Joy?

- If you read John 3:16-17, why is verse 17 often the more important to you in prayer?

A Christmas Eve Labyrinth Walk

If desired and possible in the space, the colors White or Gold are preferred for decorations, banners, ribbons, etc.

Anticipation is at its greatest on Christmas Eve, when children might be waiting for presents, but we are waiting for the greatest present of all: salvation. Jesus' name (*Yeshua* in Hebrew) is the Hebrew word for Salvation, and that point must never be lost on us.

Preparing before the Labyrinth

Sitting or standing, take a moment of quiet contemplation and then reading from John 3:16–17:

> For God so loved the world that he gave His one and only Son, that whoever believes in him shall not perish but have eternal life. For God did not send His Son into the world to condemn the world, but to save the world through him. *John 3:16–17*
>
> O God incarnate, I thank You that my time of waiting is nearly over; the anticipation of advent is like a breath about to be exhaled. Come to the Bethlehem that is my heart and restore me spiritually. Amen.

Read the following from Luke 1:26–38:

> In the sixth month the angel Gabriel was sent by God to a town in Galilee called Nazareth, to a virgin engaged to a man whose name was Joseph, of the house of David. The virgin's name was Mary. And he came to her and said, "Greetings, favored one! The Lord is with you." But she was much perplexed by his words and pondered what sort of greeting this might be. The angel said to her, "Do not be afraid, Mary, for you have found favor with God. And now, you will conceive in your womb and bear a son, and you will name him Jesus. He will be great, and will be called the Son of the Most High, and the Lord God will give to him the throne of his ancestor David. He will reign over the house of Jacob forever, and of his kingdom there will

be no end." Mary said to the angel, "How can this be, since I am a virgin?" The angel said to her, "The Holy Spirit will come upon you, and the power of the Most High will overshadow you; therefore the child to be born will be holy; he will be called Son of God. And now, your relative Elizabeth in her old age has also conceived a son; and this is the sixth month for her who was said to be barren. For nothing will be impossible with God." Then Mary said, "Here am I, the servant of the Lord; let it be with me according to your word." Then the angel departed from her.

If the service is in the evening, or inside a darkened space, candles may be given to each participant, lit from a common candle.

The Labyrinth

Begin the Labyrinth as is most expedient for that space. If you would like to, hold a candle if you can. You should consider just reciting John 3:16-17 as it appears above, or, as you are able, see if you can read Luke 1:39-46, 39-56 during the labyrinth. Avoid the candle getting too near the reading.

In those days Mary set out and went with haste to a Judean town in the hill country, where she entered the house of Zechariah and greeted Elizabeth. When Elizabeth heard Mary's greeting, the child leaped in her womb. And Elizabeth was filled with the Holy Spirit and exclaimed with a loud cry, "Blessed are you among women, and blessed is the fruit of your womb. And why has this happened to me, that the mother of my Lord comes to me? For as soon as I heard the sound of your greeting, the child in my womb leaped for joy. And blessed is she who believed that there would be a fulfillment of what was spoken to her by the Lord."

And Mary said,
     My soul magnifies the Lord,
     and my spirit rejoices in God my Savior,

for He has looked with favor on the lowliness of His servant.
Surely, from now on all generations will call me blessed;
for the Mighty One has done great things for me,
and holy is His name.
His mercy is for those who fear Him
from generation to generation.
He has shown strength with His arm;
He has scattered the proud in the thoughts of their hearts.
He has brought down the powerful from their thrones,
and lifted up the lowly;
He has filled the hungry with good things,
and sent the rich away empty.
He has helped His servant Israel,
in remembrance of His mercy,
according to the promise He made to our ancestors,
to Abraham and to his descendants forever."

And Mary remained with her about three months and then
returned to her home.

The Procession from Labyrinth into the World

Enfold me in the wings of your love, O God. Help my feet and
my heart to lead me to You. Strengthen my love for other people
so that I can love my enemies as much as my friends, knowing
all to be your children and made in your image. Encourage me
to see the miracle of the nativity and the boundless love for us
all that Jesus' birth represents. Help me to bring your love to all
the world, ever in your Holy Name I pray. *Amen.*

ROBERT J. F. ELSNER

Reflections from the Labyrinth

The pilgrimage to Bethlehem begins the pilgrimage to the ends of the earth. Christmas Eve is a moment of waiting, of the ultimate anticipation, and of an ultimate risk. Birth is about to happen. Renewal of the world is about to happen. Saving of souls is about to happen. But we tend to think about Christmas Eve in the simple, human terms of a baby about to be born. God chose one of the most common acts of the world, the birth of a baby, to be the most unusual and special moment in the history of the world. All of us were born that day. God, the creator of the Universe, decided to show us how much he loved us by becoming one with us and one of us. Imagine how difficult it would be to constrain yourself to human form if you were God: to make yourself fully human while still being fully God. Overwhelming love of humanity is just the beginning of God's motivation for this astonishing act that is lost on so many people.

Questions to ask yourself

* In the labyrinth, can you contemplate our mortal existence as compared to the immortal reality of God?

* Mary knew she would have a difficult time socially after the birth of her son, yet she submitted to God's will and the needs of the world for a savior. Where do we submit to God and serve, even when uncomfortable?

* Mary must have had some fears, but she had the Angel Gabriel to guide her. Do you have fears that block you from full acceptance of God's Love? You may not have a visible angel, but you do have God's Love Letter to you, which we call the Bible. Can scripture calm your fears?

* Where were the distraction points for you during the labyrinth that did not allow you to go as deeply into prayer as you would have liked? Could you sit and pray through those issues

elsewhere? Do you need to go and heal a relationship before you can pray more deeply?

* If you read John 3:16-17 while walking the labyrinth, did you start to focus on one part or the other? Did the necessity of verse 17 become clearer to you?

An Epiphany Walk of the Labyrinth

If desired and possible in the space, the color White is preferred for decorations, banners, ribbons, etc.

Epiphany is the remembrance of the Magi meeting the baby Jesus. This is a special walk to remind us of the constancy of meeting Jesus for the first time, as our relationship is always changing, even if Jesus never changes. We sometimes read the story of the Wedding at Cana as this is another manifestation of Jesus as God. Both are considered epiphanies and celebrated on the same day.

Preparing before the Labyrinth

Sitting or standing, take a moment of quiet contemplation and then reading from Matthew 2:1–12:

> In the time of King Herod, after Jesus was born in Bethlehem of Judea, wise men from the East came to Jerusalem, asking, "Where is the child who has been born king of the Jews? For we observed his star at its rising, and have come to pay him homage." When King Herod heard this, he was frightened, and all Jerusalem with him; and calling together all the chief priests and scribes of the people, he inquired of them where the Messiah was to be born. They told him, "In Bethlehem of Judea; for so it has been written by the prophet:
>
>> 'And you, Bethlehem, in the land of Judah,
>> are by no means least among the rulers of Judah;
>> for from you shall come a ruler
>> who is to shepherd my people Israel.'"
>
> Then Herod secretly called for the wise men and learned from them the exact time when the star had appeared. Then he sent them to Bethlehem, saying, "Go and search diligently for the child; and when you have found him, bring me word so that I may also go and pay him homage." When they had heard the king, they set out; and there, ahead of them, went the star that they had seen at its rising, until it stopped over the place where the child was. When they saw that the star had stopped, they

were overwhelmed with joy. On entering the house, they saw the child with Mary his mother; and they knelt down and paid him homage. Then, opening their treasure chests, they offered him gifts of gold, frankincense, and myrrh. And having been warned in a dream not to return to Herod, they left for their own country by another road.

Or this from the second chapter of the Gospel according to John:

[1]And the third day there was a marriage in Cana of Galilee; and the mother of Jesus was there: [2]And both Jesus was called, and his disciples, to the marriage. [3]And when they wanted wine, the mother of Jesus saith unto him, They have no wine. [4]Jesus saith unto her, Woman, what have I to do with thee? Mine hour is not yet come. [5]His mother saith unto the servants, Whatsoever he saith unto you, do it. [6]And there were set there six waterpots of stone, after the manner of the purifying of the Jews, containing two or three firkins apiece. [7]Jesus saith unto them, Fill the waterpots with water. And they filled them up to the brim. [8]And he saith unto them, Draw out now, and bear unto the governor of the feast. And they bare it. [9]When the ruler of the feast had tasted the water that was made wine, and knew not whence it was: (but the servants which drew the water knew;) the governor of the feast called the bridegroom, [10]And saith unto him, Every man at the beginning doth set forth good wine; and when men have well drunk, then that which is worse: but thou hast kept the good wine until now. [11]This beginning of miracles did Jesus in Cana of Galilee, and manifested forth his glory; and his disciples believed on him.

The Labyrinth

Begin the Labyrinth as is most expedient for that space, holding your candles if you would like. Try repeating the Lord's prayer as you journey through the labyrinth:

Our Father, who art in heaven,
      hallowed be thy Name,

thy kingdom come,
thy will be done,
> on earth as it is in heaven.
Give us this day our daily bread.
And forgive us our trespasses,
> as we forgive those who trespass against us.
And lead us not into temptation,
> but deliver us from evil.
For thine is the kingdom, and the power, and the glory,
> for ever and ever. Amen.

The Procession from Labyrinth into the World

As God appeared before Moses at the burning bush, and Christ was revealed to the world by Magi, at Cana, and at His baptism, let us remember that God is with us always. His Holy Spirit is present and enfolds us in love and peace. Share that love, peace, and presence with the world, now and always.

Reflections from the Labyrinth

This pilgrimage was awakening the recognition of God's presence in our lives. Epiphany is remembering that Jesus was with us and revealed himself as God. To the Magi, Jesus was revealed as Immanuel, God with us, to Gentiles as well as to Jews. God became incarnate for everyone, including *you*. You were thought of by God as the universe was planned and created. You were thought of and loved. Jesus came for you just as personally and intentionally as he did for the Apostles.

Questions to ask yourself

- How does God reveal himself in your life? When have you known God to really be present?

- Not everyone feels God. How could you help someone else to see Jesus in their lives?

- We don't always bring Jesus gold, frankincense, or myrrh. What are the gifts we should be bringing to lay at his feet every day?

- At the wedding feast at Cana, Jesus made lots of wine, even though people had already been drinking too much. The wine was a sign of the richness of God's blessings, even to excess. What are the blessings that are so excessive in your life that you take them for granted, or sometimes forget that they are there?

A Labyrinth Walk for the Baptism of the Lord

If desired and possible in the space, the color White is preferred for decorations, banners, ribbons, etc.

The Baptism of Jesus is a festival remembering Jesus humbling himself to be baptized by John, but also the moment of the skies splitting open and God declaring Jesus as the eternal Son of God. That moment is both an epiphany—revelation of God—but also a theophany—the visible presence of God with us, like the burning bush.

Preparing before the Labyrinth

Sitting or standing, take a moment of quiet contemplation and then reading from Matthew 3:13-17 (NRSV)

> Then Jesus came from Galilee to John at the Jordan, to be baptized by him. John would have prevented him, saying, 'I need to be baptized by you, and do you come to me?' But Jesus answered him, 'Let it be so now; for it is proper for us in this way to fulfil all righteousness.' Then he consented. And when Jesus had been baptized, just as he came up from the water, suddenly the heavens were opened to him and he saw the Spirit of God descending like a dove and alighting on him. And a voice from heaven said, 'This is my Son, the Beloved, with whom I am well pleased.'

The Labyrinth

Begin the Labyrinth as is most expedient for that space. An appropriate Baptism hymn or anthem may quietly be sung or played if desired. Among the most popular are: All my "Hope on God is Founded," "Be Thou My Vision," "Breathe on Me Breath of God," "Guide Me O Thou Great Jehovah," or "All Things Bright and Beautiful," but choose hymns to sing or to play while you walk that mean something to you. If you need a silent prayer, try something like:

Wash me though, Lord. Let me be dedicated to your love.

The Procession from Labyrinth into the World

O God, you revealed Jesus to the world as the Divine Son; help me to humbly thank You for the blessing of forgiveness and Love. Reveal to me the remembrance that I am also God's Beloved child. Wash me of pride and help me to love others and share the joy of God's love with all. *Amen.*

Reflections from the Labyrinth

In many ways, this was a pilgrimage to achieve cleanliness and the removal of sin—a feat we cannot do alone. It was not a lonely pilgrimage, but one journeyed with all the saints who have gone before us. Baptism was a tradition for some in Israel to wash themselves of sin and to repent. Though he himself was without sin, Jesus set an example for us by being baptized, demonstrating that we ought to undergo this rite to begin our journey of spiritual renewal and restoration. In the labyrinth, you journey to walk as Jesus walked, and to meet God. Perhaps the skies might not open before you, but God is still there, shining His love down upon you.

Questions to ask yourself

- Why did Jesus choose to reveal himself through an act of humility instead of an act that demonstrated his power and dominion over all the earth?

- Does God still show himself to be with us in these days, or did that stop after the Bible was written? If so, how?

- Baptism is "once-and-done," not something that needs to be repeated to wash away sin. How do we help ourselves to remember that we are forgiven, even when we do not feel like we are?

- How do you help yourself remember that God is present with you at all times?

A Labyrinth Walk for the Transfiguration

If desired and possible in the space, the color White is preferred for decorations, banners, ribbons, etc.

The Transfiguration appears in the Synoptic Gospels (Matthew 17:1-8; Mark 9:2-9; Luke 9:28-36) and recounts that Jesus went up onto a high mountain with Peter, James, and John. While there, Jesus was transformed, so that his face shone like the sun and his clothing became white as light. Moses and Elijah came down from heaven to speak with Jesus, demonstrating that Jesus was and is above even these mightiest of prophets.

Preparing before the Labyrinth

Sitting or standing, take a moment of quiet contemplation and then reading from Matthew 17:1-13:

> Six days later, Jesus took with him Peter and James and his brother John and led them up a high mountain, by themselves. And he was transfigured before them, and his face shone like the sun, and his clothes became dazzling white. Suddenly there appeared to them Moses and Elijah, talking with him. Then Peter said to Jesus, 'Lord, it is good for us to be here; if you wish, I will make three dwellings here, one for you, one for Moses, and one for Elijah.' While he was still speaking, suddenly a bright cloud overshadowed them, and from the cloud a voice said, 'This is my Son, the Beloved; with him I am well pleased; listen to him!' When the disciples heard this, they fell to the ground and were overcome by fear. But Jesus came and touched them, saying, 'Get up and do not be afraid.' And when they looked up, they saw no one except Jesus himself alone. As they were coming down the mountain, Jesus ordered them, Tell no one about the vision until after the Son of Man has been raised from the dead.' And the disciples asked him, 'Why, then, do the scribes say that Elijah must come first?' He replied, 'Elijah is indeed coming and will restore all things; but I tell you that Elijah has already come, and they did not recognize him, but they

did to him whatever they pleased. So also the Son of Man is about to suffer at their hands.' Then the disciples understood that he was speaking to them about John the Baptist.

The Labyrinth

Begin the Labyrinth as is most expedient for that space. An appropriate hymn or anthem may quietly be sung if desired. Focus on the humanity and divinity of Jesus should be emphasized. Alternatively, the following prayer may be repeated while journeying the labyrinth:

O Lord, bless me so that I may see You in my life.

Lord, transform my heart and mind.

Bless all the countries of the Earth, and let peace prevail among all people.

Lord, transform my heart and mind.

Strengthen me to withstand doubt and fear and walk in your ways.

Lord, transform my heart and mind.

Help me to understand You, O God, and write your Laws in my heart.

Lord, transform my heart and mind.

The Procession from Labyrinth into the World

O Christ, you showed yourself with Moses and Elijah to Peter, James, and John; let me know you and see you in my life. Help me to ever remember that you were fully human, yet also fully divine. Enfold me in your radiant love and transfigure my heart and mind to love and serve you and be kinder to others. In your Holy Name I pray. *Amen.*

Reflections from the Labyrinth

This journey was a pilgrimage of hope and shows that we too can be transfigured. Too often we focus on our lost potential instead of the amazing blessings and opportunities God has bestowed on us. Each day that we wake up is another day to worship God and love other people, even when they might be disagreeable and difficult to love. Allow yourself to be transformed to hear God always.

Questions to ask yourself

* How do you need to be transformed in your life? What would that transformation look like if you were holy and dedicated to God?

* Have you ever seen anyone go through a transformation that makes them a different or better person? Were the transformative moments positive, negative, or both?

* Do you need to see Moses and Elijah come down from the sky to understand the presence of God in your life?

* Can your life actually be so transformed such that you can listen for God, even when it appears that only silence prevails?

CHAPTER 4

LENTEN LABYRINTH WALKS

L ent is a term that literally means lengthening, a reference to the longer days of spring. Lent is a church season of repentance and reflection as we move from the cold and dark of our hearts to the great joy of our salvation that culminates in Easter.

Beginning with Ash Wednesday, Lent is forty days long. It is solemn, yet there is joy reflected in the time of prayer and worship. Remember that joy is an internal feeling of internal selfless contentment and peace, and that is part of the goal of these labyrinth journeys. The darkest days help us to see the light and brightness of our salvation through Jesus on that Glorious Easter morning.

An Ash Wednesday Labyrinth Walk

If desired and possible in the space, the color Violet (or unbleached linen) is preferred for decorations, banners, ribbons, etc.

On Ash Wednesday we are reminded of the brevity of life and how quickly the seasons of life can change. Ash Wednesday is the first day of the Lenten season in which we think about Jesus going slowly to Jerusalem to die upon the cross. We are poor in many ways, even if we are rich in others.

Preparing before the Labyrinth

Sitting or standing, take a moment of quiet contemplation and then reading from Matthew 6:1-6, 16-21:

> Beware of practicing your piety before others in order to be seen by them; for then you have no reward from your Father in heaven. So whenever you give alms, do not sound a trumpet before you, as the hypocrites do in the synagogues and in the streets, so that they may be praised by others. Truly I tell you, they have received their reward. But when you give alms, do not let your left hand know what your right hand is doing, so that your alms may be done in secret; and your Father who sees in secret will reward you. And whenever you pray, do not be like the hypocrites; for they love to stand and pray in the synagogues and at the street corners, so that they may be seen by others. Truly I tell you, they have received their reward. But whenever you pray, go into your room and shut the door and pray to your Father who is in secret; and your Father who sees in secret will reward you. And whenever you fast, do not look dismal, like the hypocrites, for they disfigure their faces so as to show others that they are fasting. Truly I tell you, they have received their reward. But when you fast, put oil on your head and wash your face, so that your fasting may be seen not by others but by your Father who is in secret; and your Father who sees in secret will reward you. Do not store up for yourselves

treasures on earth, where moth and rust consume and where thieves break in and steal; but store up for yourselves treasures in heaven, where neither moth nor rust consumes and where thieves do not break in and steal. For where your treasure is, there your heart will be also.

The Labyrinth

If you are not alone, a foot washing is appropriate. It can be especially poignant to walk the labyrinth barefoot if you are able and the weather permits. If you are using a finger-tracing labyrinth, consider having ash or soil on it so that you need to wash your hands afterwards. Begin the Labyrinth as is most expedient for that space. If you are able, read Psalm 51, at least verses 1-17, during the journey.

Have mercy on me, O God, according to your steadfast love;
according to your abundant mercy blot out my transgressions.
Wash me thoroughly from my iniquity, and cleanse me from
my sin.
For I know my transgressions, and my sin is ever before me.
Against You, you alone, have I sinned, and done what is evil in
your sight, so that you are justified in your sentence and
blameless when You pass judgment.
Indeed, I was born guilty, a sinner when my mother conceived
me.
You desire truth in the inward being; therefore teach me
wisdom in my secret heart.
Purge me with hyssop, and I shall be clean; wash me, and I
shall be whiter than snow.
Let me hear joy and gladness; let the bones that You have
crushed rejoice.
Hide your face from my sins, and blot out all my iniquities.
Create in me a clean heart, O God, and put a new and right
spirit within me.
Do not cast me away from your presence, and do not take your
holy spirit from me.

Restore to me the joy of your salvation, and sustain in me a
willing spirit.
Then I will teach transgressors your ways, and sinners will
return to You.
Deliver me from bloodshed, O God, O God of my salvation,
and my tongue will sing aloud of your deliverance.
O Lord, open my lips, and my mouth will declare your praise.
For You have no delight in sacrifice; if I were to give a burnt
offering, You would not be pleased.
The sacrifice acceptable to God is a broken spirit; a broken and
contrite heart, O God, You will not despise.

The Procession from Labyrinth into the World

Bless me and keep me, Lord of Love, Peace, and Mercy. Where my
spirit is tainted, cleanse me and let purity redefine my life. Where I
have a disregard for the lives of others, remind me of my own mortality and your promise of eternal life. Strengthen me to serve and love
You that with my last breath I praise You. Amen.

Reflections from the Labyrinth

On this first day of the Lenten season, we focus on our mortality.
The ashes that last year were used to symbolize Christ's triumphant
entry to Jerusalem are now used to remind us that we will return to
dust, and that all we build will one day be reduced to ash. This tradition is not meant to be morbid, but to be hopeful, reminding us that
what we see and value here are merely glimmers of what we will see
in God's Kingdom.

Questions to ask yourself

- Why might some people fear or be embarrassed by Ash Wednesday? How does that fear play into your life?

- How do ashes help you to remember your own mortality without evoking fear?

- What are sources of hopefulness in the remembrance of this day?

A Lenten Labyrinth Walk

If desired and possible in the space, the color Violet (or unbleached linen) is preferred for decorations, banners, ribbons, etc.

Lent is a church tradition based on the temptation of Christ in the wilderness as he prepared for the end of his earthly life and ministry *(Mark 1:13; Matthew 4:1–11; Luke 4:1–13).* The season is supposed to be used to focus on the blessings we have at the expense of Jesus' sacrifice and the great loving-kindness of God. While some people focus on the traditions of giving up material things like certain foods, others focus on the giving up of spiritual burdens like hatred, arrogance, envy, and other emotions that tear us away from God.

Preparing before the Labyrinth

Sitting or standing, take a moment of quiet contemplation and then reading from 1 Kings 19:

> ⁹There Elijah entered a cave and spent the night. And the word of the LORD came to him, saying, "What are you doing here, Elijah?"
>
> ¹⁰"I have been very zealous for the LORD, the God of Hosts," he replied, "but the Israelites have forsaken Your covenant, torn down Your altars, and killed Your prophets with the sword. I am the only one left, and they are seeking my life as well."
>
> ¹¹Then the LORD said, "Go out and stand on the mountain before the LORD. Behold, the LORD is about to pass by."
>
> And a great and mighty wind tore into the mountains and shattered the rocks before the LORD, but the LORD was not in the wind.
>
> After the wind there was an earthquake, but the LORD was not in the earthquake.
>
> ¹²After the earthquake there was a fire, but the LORD was not in the fire.

And after the fire came a still, small voice. [13]When Elijah heard it, he wrapped his face in his cloak and went out and stood at the mouth of the cave. Suddenly a voice came to him and said, "What are you doing here, Elijah?"

Jesus, remind me of your presence in the dark times through your soft, small voice as well as through thunder and earthquakes. Embrace me, O God, with protection from myself as well as from others. When I have plenty, help me to share. When I have nothing, help me to have hope and learn what I truly need. Help me journey through this labyrinth in the safety of your enduring love. Amen.

The Labyrinth

Begin the Labyrinth as is most expedient for that space. As you begin the Labyrinth, try reading Psalm 51 in its entirety and repeat the first lines as needed:

Have mercy on me, O God,
according to your steadfast love;
according to your abundant mercy,
blot out my transgressions.
Wash me thoroughly from my iniquity,
and cleanse me from my sin.
For I know my transgressions,
and my sin is ever before me.
Against You, You alone, have I sinned
and done what is evil in your sight,
so that You are justified in your sentence
and blameless when You pass judgment.
Indeed, I was born guilty,
a sinner when my mother conceived me.
You desire truth in the inward being;
therefore teach me wisdom in my secret heart.
Purge me with hyssop, and I shall be clean;
wash me, and I shall be whiter than snow.

Let me hear joy and gladness;
let the bones that You have crushed rejoice.
Hide your face from my sins,
and blot out all my iniquities.
Create in me a clean heart, O God,
and put a new and right spirit within me.
Do not cast me away from your presence,
and do not take your holy spirit from me.
Restore to me the joy of your salvation,
and sustain in me a willing spirit.
Then I will teach transgressors your ways,
and sinners will return to You.
Deliver me from bloodshed, O God,
O God of my salvation,
and my tongue will sing aloud of your deliverance.
O Lord, open my lips,
and my mouth will declare your praise.
For You have no delight in sacrifice;
if I were to give a burnt offering, You would not be pleased.
The sacrifice acceptable to God is a broken spirit;
a broken and contrite heart, O God, You will not despise.
Do good to Zion in your good pleasure;
rebuild the walls of Jerusalem;
then You will delight in right sacrifices,
in burnt offerings and whole burnt offerings;
then bulls will be offered on your altar.

The Procession from Labyrinth into the World

If we say that we have no sin, we deceive ourselves, and the truth is not in us. If we confess our sins, he who is faithful and just will forgive us our sins and cleanse us from all unrighteousness. If we say that we have not sinned, we make Him a liar, and His word is not in us. *1 John 1:8-10*

O Lord, let me be blessed fully and in humility. You are the one who made me and loves me as I am. Help me to repent from sins I know about, and those I cannot see. Empower me, O God, to forgive others of whatever I hold against them. Remind me always that the blessings of the Father, Son, and Holy Spirit are with me now and always. Amen.

Reflections from the Labyrinth

During Lent, we tend to focus on ourselves, whether it is our hunger, our inconvenience, or our pain. Lent is about focusing on God instead of focusing on ourselves. In the midst of the labyrinth, if you can, seek the presence of God, even when we cannot hear His voice. Feel the world around you emotionally and spiritually as well as physically. Is there evidence of love and peace, even if we are preparing to die as Jesus was during this period? He knew he was going to die, and he continued to heal, reconcile, and even washed feet, which is a dirty, humbling task. He offered forgiveness, even to those who betrayed and forsook him.

Questions to ask yourself

- Do you really sin without knowing it? If you don't know that what you have done is sinful, is it really sin?

- What should you be giving up for Lent, and should you pick those things back up after Lent is over?

- What do you really get from observing Lent? Is it simply written up in a divine ledger, or is it supposed to be much more meaningful?

A Palm Sunday Labyrinth Walk

If desired and possible in the space, the color Red is preferred for decorations, banners, ribbons, etc.

Palm Sunday commemorates Jesus' triumphant entrance into Jerusalem. It was an anxious time for everyone, as the Jews had just proclaimed Jesus as their King—a point of controversy among the Romans who had a king of their own. People lined the road with their clothes and palm leaves to pave the way for Jesus. In the labyrinth, we too are preparing for the coming of Jesus as he makes his way into our heart.

Preparing before the Labyrinth

Sitting or standing, take a moment of quiet contemplation and then reading from John 12:12-16

> The great crowd that had come to the festival heard that Jesus was coming to Jerusalem. So they took branches of palm trees and went out to meet him, shouting, "Hosanna! Blessed is the one who comes in the name of the Lord-- the King of Israel!" Jesus found a young donkey and sat on it; as it is written: "Do not be afraid, daughter of Zion. Look, your king is coming, sitting on a donkey's colt!" His disciples did not understand these things at first; but when Jesus was glorified, then they remembered that these things had been written of him and had been done to him.

> I thank you and praise You, Almighty God, for the overwhelming love You give me and by which you redeemed the world through Christ. On this day Jesus entered the holy city of Jerusalem in triumph and was proclaimed as King of kings by those who spread their garments and branches of palm along his way. Let the branches I carry through this Labyrinth be for me a sign of his victory and a reminder of his carrying the cross for our salvation. Grant that I can really feel bearing them in his name that I can ever hail him as King and follow him in the way that leads to eternal life. Amen.

The Labyrinth

Begin the Labyrinth as is most expedient for that space, carrying palms if possible. Songs of praise and Hosannas should be sung, even if just in your head.

The Procession from Labyrinth into the World

O God our King, I know that you came in humility to save me from sin and death. Help me to do the equivalent of throwing cloaks and palms on the road before you to soften your journey and honor your approach to where I live. Please help me to not hide my faith or use my faith to hurt others. Let me wholeheartedly welcome you into my heart and home, now and always. *Amen.*

Reflections from the Labyrinth

Palm Sunday is often misunderstood. In the lectionary reading from Mark 11, villagers threw their cloaks and leafy branches on the road to make way for Jesus. During this time period, the road was covered with dust, dirt, and garbage, and clothes were expensive and precious. For people to be so overwhelmed with love to honor Jesus by paving his way with their own clothes is far beyond what most of us could ever understand. In our own hearts, we should try to focus on what we give to God, and not just what we can afford. It is not just about money. It is about our time, our energy, and our focus. If this is too hard to think through in other ways, start with thinking about money: What is more precious to God is not your money, but your mind. If God is not in your thoughts often, then that is where you should start making changes in your life. This frees us to focus on other people and become kinder and more generous.

Questions to ask yourself

- If you give to the church or to charities, do you give enough to notice? Do you give enough to have to budget your giving? If you budget, do you give so much that it hurts because tough decisions have to be made?

- What do you focus on and think about most? How can you start to position God more in your mind so that you worry less about yourself and more about others who are beloved of God?

A Maundy Thursday Labyrinth Walk

If desired and possible in the space, the color Red is preferred for decorations, banners, ribbons, etc.

Maundy Thursday is the remembrance of the Passover feast that was Christ's last. At this feast, famously known as the Last Supper, the Lord was betrayed, denied, and abandoned by most. Fortunately for us, we have a God who experienced the many trials and tribulations of life and can help us as we undergo our own.

Preparing before the Labyrinth

Sitting or standing, take a moment of quiet contemplation before reading from Psalm 116:1-2, 12-19

> I love the LORD, because He has heard my voice and my
> supplications.
> Because He inclined His ear to me, therefore I will call on Him
> as long as I live.
> What shall I return to the LORD for all His bounty to me?
> I will lift up the cup of salvation and call on the name of the LORD,
> I will pay my vows to the LORD in the presence of all His people.
> Precious in the sight of the LORD is the death of His faithful
> ones.
> O LORD, I am your servant; I am your servant, the child of
> your serving girl.
> You have loosed my bonds.
> I will offer to you a thanksgiving sacrifice and call on the name
> of the LORD.
> I will pay my vows to the LORD in the presence of all His people,
> in the courts of the house of the LORD, in your midst, O
> Jerusalem.
> Praise the LORD!

If you have time, please read the Gospel according to John 13:1-17, 31b-35:

> Now before the festival of the Passover, Jesus knew that
> his hour had come to depart from this world and go to the

Father. Having loved his own who were in the world, he loved them to the end. The devil had already put it into the heart of Judas son of Simon Iscariot to betray him. And during supper Jesus, knowing that the Father had given all things into his hands, and that he had come from God and was going to God, got up from the table, took off his outer robe, and tied a towel around himself. Then he poured water into a basin and began to wash the disciples' feet and to wipe them with the towel that was tied around him. He came to Simon Peter, who said to him, "Lord, are you going to wash my feet?" Jesus answered, "You do not know now what I am doing, but later you will understand." Peter said to him, "You will never wash my feet." Jesus answered, "Unless I wash you, you have no share with me." Simon Peter said to him, "Lord, not my feet only but also my hands and my head!" Jesus said to him, "One who has bathed does not need to wash, except for the feet, but is entirely clean. And you are clean, though not all of you." For he knew who was to betray him; for this reason he said, "Not all of you are clean." After he had washed their feet, had put on his robe, and had returned to the table, he said to them, "Do you know what I have done to you? You call me Teacher and Lord--and you are right, for that is what I am. So if I, your Lord and Teacher, have washed your feet, you also ought to wash one another's feet. For I have set you an example, that you also should do as I have done to you. Very truly, I tell you, servants are not greater than their master, nor are messengers greater than the one who sent them. If you know these things, you are blessed if you do them." When he had gone out, Jesus said, "Now the Son of Man has been glorified, and God has been glorified in him. If God has been glorified in him, God will also glorify him in himself and will glorify him at once. Little children, I am with you only a little longer. You will look for me; and as I said to the Jews so now I say to you, 'Where I am going, you cannot come.' I give you a new commandment, that you love one another. Just as I have loved you, you also should love one another. By this everyone will know that you are my disciples, if you have love for one another."

The Labyrinth

A foot washing is appropriate if you are walking with other people. Begin the Labyrinth as is most expedient for that space. If possible, silence should be kept except for quiet prayers. As you journey through, try to focus on both the trials and tribulations of your life, but also the hope of resolution and advance in faith that those tend to bring. If you need a helpful phrase to repeat, consider:

Lord, help me through my trials and tribulations to strengthen my faith. Teach me to love others as you love us.

The Procession from Labyrinth into the World

Blessed are the feet of the messengers who bring us the gospel of peace. Spirit of Light and Life, shine on my path so I can see love and forgiveness for the betrayals in my life. God of Love and Kindness who led Israel to the Promised Land, please guide me to Peace and reconciliation. Jesus, who washed feet as a servant, please rule over my heart so that I may serve others. God, Father, Son, and Holy Spirit, be with me and stay with me now and always. *Amen.*

Reflections from the Labyrinth

Maundy Thursday is a day of remembrance and forgiveness. Jesus was abandoned by most of his disciples, completely betrayed by one, and falsely accused of many crimes. It was a sad day. Yet, it was also a day of beauty, when Jesus—who knew all that was about to happen—not only had dinner one last time with his friends but also reminded them that he was there to serve, going down on his knees and washing their feet, a duty relegated solely to the lowest of servants. What a great reminder of the importance of service and that great things can come from our worst moments.

Questions to ask yourself

- If you are facing bad times, do you remember to serve others in some way or other?
- How can you focus your attention on God so that you put your trust in God more than you worry on other people?
- Do you listen to the good messages as much as the bad messages that you hear?

A Good Friday Labyrinth Walk

If desired and possible in the space, the colors Black or Red are preferred for decorations, banners, ribbons, etc.

Many have decried the name Good Friday, as it is difficult at first to see the good in it. After all, it is the day of pain and suffering—when Jesus, our Lord, succumbed on the cross. However, we must remember that Good Friday is indeed *good*, for it is the day when Jesus demonstrated the unconditional and all-powerful love of God and saved us from our sins.

Preparing before the Labyrinth

Sitting or standing, take a moment of quiet contemplation before reading from Jeremiah 31:33:

> But this is the covenant that I will make with the house of Israel after those days, says the Lord: I will put my law within them, and I will write it on their hearts; and I will be their God, and they shall be my people.

> GOD spoke these words, and said: I am the LORD thy God; Thou shalt have none other gods but me.

Lord, have mercy upon me, and incline my heart to keep this law.

> Thou shalt not make to thyself any graven image, nor the likeness of any thing that is in heaven above, or in the earth beneath, or in the water under the earth; thou shalt not bow down to them, nor worship them: for I the Lord thy God am a jealous God, and visit the sins of the fathers upon the children, unto the third and fourth generation of them that hate me; and show mercy unto thousands in them that love me and keep my commandments.

Lord, have mercy upon me, and incline my heart to keep this law.

> Thou shalt not take the Name of the Lord thy God in vain; for the Lord will not hold him guiltless, that taketh His Name in vain.

Lord, have mercy upon me, and incline my heart to keep this law.

Remember that thou keep holy the Sabbath-day. Six days shalt thou labour, and do all that thou hast to do; but the seventh day is the Sabbath of the Lord thy God. In it thou shalt do no manner of work; thou, and thy son, and thy daughter, thy man-servant, and thy maid-servant, thy cattle, and the stranger that is within thy gates. For in six days the Lord made heaven and earth, the sea, and all that in them is, and rested the seventh day: wherefore the Lord blessed the seventh day, and hallowed it.

Lord, have mercy upon me, and incline my heart to keep this law.

Honor thy father and thy mother; that thy days may be long in the land which the Lord thy God giveth thee.

Lord, have mercy upon me, and incline my heart to keep this law.

Thou shalt do no murder.

Lord, have mercy upon me, and incline my heart to keep this law.

Thou shalt not commit adultery.

Lord, have mercy upon me, and incline my heart to keep this law.

Thou shalt not steal.

Lord, have mercy upon me, and incline my heart to keep this law.

Thou shalt not bear false witness against thy neighbor.

Lord, have mercy upon me, and incline my heart to keep this law.

Thou shalt not covet thy neighbor's house, thou shalt not covet thy neighbor's wife, nor his servant, nor his maid, nor his ox, nor his ass, nor any thing that is his.

Lord, have mercy upon me, and incline my heart to keep this law.

Hear what our Lord Jesus Christ saith. Thou shalt love the Lord thy God with all thy heart, and with all thy soul, and with all thy mind. This is the first and great commandment. And the second is like unto it; Thou shalt love thy neighbor as thyself. On these two commandments hang all the Law and the Prophets.

Lord, have mercy upon me, and incline my heart to keep this law.

The Labyrinth

Begin to journey the Labyrinth as is most expedient for that space. As you go, read or listen to Psalm 22 in its entirety:

My God, my God, why have You forsaken me?
Why are You so far from saving me, so far from my words of
    groaning?
I cry out by day, O my God, but You do not answer,
and by night, but I have no rest.
Yet You are holy, enthroned on the praises of Israel.
In You our fathers trusted; they trusted and You delivered them.
They cried out to You and were set free;
they trusted in You and were not disappointed.
But I am a worm and not a man, scorned by men and despised
    by the people.
All who see me mock me; they sneer and shake their heads:
"He trusts in the LORD, let the LORD deliver him;
let the LORD rescue him, since He delights in him."
Yet You brought me forth from the womb;
You made me secure at my mother's breast.
From birth I was cast upon You; from my mother's womb You
    have been my God.
Be not far from me, for trouble is near and there is no one to
    help.

Many bulls surround me; strong bulls of Bashan encircle me.

They open their jaws against me like lions that roar and maul.

I am poured out like water, and all my bones are disjointed.

My heart is like wax; it melts away within me.

My strength is dried up like a potsherd, and my tongue sticks
to the roof of my mouth.

You lay me in the dust of death.

For dogs surround me; a band of evil men encircles me; they
have pierced my hands and feet.

I can count all my bones; they stare and gloat over me.

They divide my garments among them and cast lots for my
clothing.

But You, O LORD, be not far off; O my Strength, come
quickly to help me.

Deliver my soul from the sword, my precious life from the
power of wild dogs.

Save me from the mouth of the lion; at the horns of the wild
oxen

You have answered me!

I will proclaim Your name to my brothers; I will praise You in
the assembly.

You who fear the LORD, praise Him! All descendants of Jacob,
honor Him!

All offspring of Israel, revere Him!

For He has not despised or detested the torment of the
afflicted.

He has not hidden His face from him, but has attended to his
cry for help.

My praise for You resounds in the great assembly; I will fulfill
my vows before those who fear You.

The poor will eat and be satisfied; those who seek the LORD
will praise Him.

May your hearts live forever!

All the ends of the earth will remember and turn to the LORD.

All the families of the nations will bow down before Him.

For dominion belongs to the LORD and He rules over the
    nations.
All the rich of the earth will feast and worship; all who go
    down to the dust will kneel before Him—
even those unable to preserve their lives.
Posterity will serve Him; they will declare the Lord to a new
    generation.
They will come and proclaim His righteousness to a people yet
    unborn—all that He has done.

The Procession from Labyrinth into the World

Love does no wrong to a neighbor; therefore, love is the fulfilling of the law. *-Romans 13:10*

O, Almighty Lord, and everlasting God, we beseech thee to
direct, sanctify, and govern, both our hearts and bodies, in the
ways of thy laws, and in the works of thy commandments; that,
through thy most mighty protection, both here and ever, we may
be preserved in body and soul; through our Lord and Savior
Jesus Christ. *Amen.*

Reflections from the Labyrinth

Sometimes people say that there is no good in Good Friday. The
death of our Lord and Savior can be troubling to everyone—even
people of faith. But, without Jesus' crucifixion, we would never realize
just how truly God understands our fears, pains, and sufferings or
even our hopes, joys, and dreams. Through his death, Jesus showed us
that death is not the end, but rather a transition point to a new life.

Questions to ask yourself

- Have you ever read the entirety of Psalm 22, a psalm about Jesus? What does the psalm really mean to Good Friday?

    o Was Jesus feeling forsaken, or did he want people to remember that His hope was always in God and that God was being glorified by the crucifixion?

- How can we build our faith, even in the sight of horrible pain and suffering?

A Holy Saturday Labyrinth Walk

If desired and possible in the space, the colors White or Gold are preferred for decorations, banners, ribbons, etc.

Holy Saturday is the ultimate day of contemplation and mourning that is also balanced with joyful expectation. While we mourn the death of Jesus, we also anticipate His resurrection and the conquering of death itself. It is a day of intense faith and focus.

Preparing before the Labyrinth

Sitting or standing, take a moment of quiet contemplation.

> I believe in the sun even when it is not shining,
> I believe in love even when I cannot feel it,
> I believe in God even when He is silent.[1]

Focus on the meaning of that poem before engaging with this reading from Deuteronomy 5:6-18

> I, Yahweh, am your God who brought you out of the land of Egypt, the house of bondage: You shall have no other gods beside Me.

> You shall not make for yourself a sculptured image, any likeness of what is in the heavens above, or on the earth below, or in the waters below the earth. You shall not bow down to them or serve them. For I your God Yahweh am an impassioned God, visiting the guilt of the parents upon the children, upon the third and upon the fourth generations of those who reject Me, but showing kindness to the thousandth generation of those who love Me and keep My commandments.

> Lead me in your Way, O Lord, and write your Law in my heart.

> You shall not swear falsely by the name of your God Yahweh; for Yahweh will not clear one who swears falsely by God's name.

> Lead me in your Way, O Lord, and write your Law in my heart.

---

1. written on a prison cell wall at Auschwitz during the Holocaust

Observe the sabbath day and keep it holy, as your God Yahweh has commanded you. Six days you shall labor and do all your work, but the seventh day is a sabbath of your God Yahweh; you shall not do any work—you, your son or your daughter, your male or female slave, your ox or your ass, or any of your cattle, or the stranger in your settlements, so that your male and female slave may rest as you do. Remember that you were a slave in the land of Egypt and your God Yahweh freed you from there with a mighty hand and an outstretched arm; therefore your God Yahweh has commanded you to observe the sabbath day.

Lead me in your Way, O Lord, and write your Law in my heart.

Honor your father and your mother, as your God Yahweh has commanded you, that you may long endure, and that you may fare well, in the land that your God Yahweh is assigning to you.

Lead me in your Way, O Lord, and write your Law in my heart.

You shall not murder.

Lead me in your Way, O Lord, and write your Law in my heart.

You shall not commit adultery.

Lead me in your Way, O Lord, and write your Law in my heart.

You shall not steal.

Lead me in your Way, O Lord, and write your Law in my heart.

You shall not bear false witness against your neighbor.

Lead me in your Way, O Lord, and write your Law in my heart.

You shall not covet your neighbor's wife. Likewise, none of you shall crave your neighbor's house, or field, or male or female slave, or ox, or ass, or anything that is your neighbor's.

Your Way is Love, O God. Lead me in your Way, O Lord, and write your Law in my heart.

The Labyrinth

Now begin the Labyrinth as is most expedient for that space. As you progress, quietly repeat:

> Your Way is Love, O God. Lead me in your Way, and write your Law in my heart.

If there is a reason why you could not repeat that phrase, or if desired at the center of the labyrinth, read from 1 Peter 3: 13-22:

> Now who will harm you if you are eager to do what is good? But even if you do suffer for doing what is right, you are blessed. Do not fear what they fear, and do not be intimidated, but in your hearts sanctify Christ as Lord. Always be ready to make your defense to anyone who demands from you an accounting for the hope that is in you, yet do it with gentleness and respect. Maintain a good conscience so that, when you are maligned, those who abuse you for your good conduct in Christ may be put to shame. For it is better to suffer for doing good, if suffering should be God's will, than to suffer for doing evil. For Christ also suffered for sins once for all, the righteous for the unrighteous, in order to bring you to God. He was put to death in the flesh but made alive in the spirit, in which also he went and made a proclamation to the spirits in prison, who in former times did not obey, when God waited patiently in the days of Noah, during the building of the ark, in which a few, that is, eight lives, were saved through water. And baptism, which this prefigured, now saves you—not as a removal of dirt from the body but as an appeal to God for a good conscience, through the resurrection of Jesus Christ, who has gone into heaven and is at the right hand of God, with angels, authorities, and powers made subject to him.

At the conclusion of the labyrinth, pray:

> Our Father, who art in heaven,
> hallowed be thy Name,

thy kingdom come,
thy will be done,
    on earth as it is in heaven.
Give us this day our daily bread.
And forgive us our trespasses,
    as we forgive those who trespass against us.
And lead us not into temptation,
    but deliver us from evil.
For thine is the kingdom, and the power, and the glory,
    for ever and ever. Amen.

The Procession from Labyrinth into the World

O God, who led the people of Israel out of Egypt and provided the Law to set them free, write your law of love in my heart. Help me through the winding desert paths of our lives, such that I find Your Way of love mapped out in my heart. Remind me always that while Jesus was in the tomb, it was for the purpose of ending death and suffering and preparing us for new life in you. As Christ proclaimed salvation even to those who had died, let me hear the Good News while still alive and receive your blessings of life eternal.

Reflections from the Labyrinth

Holy Saturday is sometimes thought of as a sad or depressing day. It is somber and understated so that we focus on the importance of Jesus' suffering and death. We remember that Jesus' birth, life, death, resurrection, and ascension are all for our sake, bringing us to life eternal. This is a day of extraordinary hope, knowing that God wins the struggle over death. All things are possible with God, and the focus of God is on loving you.

Questions to ask yourself

- What rules apply to Jesus that might challenge what you have been taught?

- Jesus told the thief on the cross that he would be with Jesus in paradise that same day. What does that mean for you and your forgiveness?

- Where was Jesus while he was dead, and what was he doing while in the tomb?

CHAPTER 5

EASTER SEASON
LABYRINTH WALKS

E aster is one of the two definitive seasons of the Christian year. Easter is the day of atonement and redemption of the world by Jesus, breaking the power of death.

In 1 Peter 1:3, we are told that Easter is a moment when he has given us new birth into a living hope through the resurrection of Jesus Christ from the dead. In this section, the joy of salvation and the hopefulness of Easter should be a continual theme.

An Easter Labyrinth Walk

If desired and possible in the space, the colors White or Gold are preferred for decorations, banners, ribbons, etc.

Easter, like Christmas, is one of the central and most important feasts in the Church. Easter is the ultimate day of hope, wherein death itself was defeated forever. Jesus, who was fully human and fully divine—as difficult as that is to reconcile—died and then came back from the dead to show us that even death is not the end. Death is not the ruler of life; *God is.*

Preparing before the Labyrinth

Sitting or standing, take a moment of quiet contemplation and then:

O Lord, whose death upon the cross was not the end, but the beginning of a new Day and Age for us all, grant us the ability to fully praise you and come into relation with you that our hearts may be filled and overflow with your love, praising you with our hearts, our minds, and our lives. Help us to overcome our fear of death and the grave, so that we see life everlasting through You. May our time together be focused on you in true worship and lead us to that Holy Country where with all the Saints we may only see You.

The Labyrinth

Begin the Labyrinth journey as is most expedient for that space. As you are about to begin, start with this prayer:

You loved us enough to die for us, and loved us even more, so overcame death and lived for us.

Repeat as you journey:

Your Way is Love, O God. Lead me in your Way and write your Law in my heart. I shall not fear death, but live for your glory.

The Procession from Labyrinth into the World

Our Father, who art in heaven,
    hallowed be thy Name,
    thy kingdom come,
    thy will be done,
        on earth as it is in heaven.
Give us this day our daily bread.
And forgive us our trespasses,
    as we forgive those who trespass against us.
And lead us not into temptation,
    but deliver us from evil.
For thine is the kingdom, and the power, and the glory,
    for ever and ever. Amen.

Let my heart be light and filled with joy. Lord, please let the remembrance of Christ's Birth, Life, Death, Resurrection, and Ascension fill me with hope. May the Risen Lord be with me throughout this and every day. Help me to focus my faith and build relationships in His Name. And may the Peace of the Lord be with me and all I love now and forever. *Amen.*

He is Risen! Thanks be to God. Alleluia!

Reflections from the Labyrinth

There is a scary contradiction of Easter to some people. We build our faith upon this idea that death is not eternal, and that it has been conquered. This is important, as it is among the most difficult ideas to wrap our very human heads around. Jesus died a painful and humiliating death on the cross and was stabbed with a spear to make sure he died. Then he came back. He came back because he loved us more than we can imagine and continues to live for us and invite us to live and love forever in and with him. There is nothing more hopeful than this simple act. He lived after he died.

Questions to ask yourself

- What doubts do you have about the resurrection story as it is written in the bible? Why might you have those doubts?

- What does it mean to you in your everyday life that Jesus came back from the dead?

- Why do some people not believe that we will all be resurrected at some point in the future after we have died in this life? How can you help those people (or yourself)?

An Ascension Day Labyrinth Walk

If desired and possible in the space, the color White is preferred for decorations, banners, ribbons, etc.

Ascension Day commemorates the day when the resurrected Jesus returned to Heaven in front of all of the disciples. Even though they were blessed to be witnesses of such an amazing event, the disciples had doubts. Indeed, to doubt is to be human, and Ascension Day is an enduring reminder that faith is a process and will always be tested.

Preparing before the Labyrinth

Sitting or standing, take a moment of quiet contemplation and then reads The Great Commission (Matthew 28:16–20, KJV):

> Then the eleven disciples went away into Galilee, into a mountain where Jesus had appointed them. And when they saw him, they worshipped him: but some doubted. And Jesus came and spake unto them, saying, All power is given unto me in heaven and in earth. Go ye therefore, and teach all nations, baptizing them in the name of the Father, and of the Son, and of the Holy Ghost: Teaching them to observe all things whatsoever I have commanded you: and, lo, I am with you always, even unto the end of the world. Amen.

The Labyrinth

Begin the Labyrinth as is most expedient for that space. As you progress through the labyrinth, pray with words about the ascension and the presence of the Holy Spirit. If you would like, repeat a solemn phrase like: "Lord Jesus, be with me on Earth as my spirit will be with you in Heaven."

The Procession from Labyrinth into the World

> Our Father, who art in heaven,
> > hallowed be thy Name,
> > thy kingdom come,

thy will be done,
on earth as it is in heaven.
Give us this day our daily bread.
And forgive us our trespasses,
as we forgive those who trespass against us.
And lead us not into temptation,
but deliver us from evil.
For thine is the kingdom, and the power, and the glory,
for ever and ever. Amen.

Alleluia, He is Risen from the dead and Risen to the Skies. Praise be to you, Holy Spirit, who remains with us to guide, comfort, and bless. With all the saints above and below, please, God bless me, Jesus strengthen me, and may the Spirit of Truth comfort me now and always. Alleluia, Alleluia. *Amen.*

Reflections from the Labyrinth

When Jesus ascended to Heaven, we were not left alone. He sent the Holy Spirit to us to comfort and guide us. What a powerful and wonderful reassurance! As you journey the labyrinth, there should be moments when you embrace the presence of the Comforter and recognize how he leads and strengthens you in your daily life.

Questions to ask yourself

- Why is it so important that Jesus ascended into Heaven? Why did he not just grow old really slowly and die to go back?

- How does the Holy Spirit provide comfort in your life? How do you listen or look for that?

A Pentecost Labyrinth Walk

If desired and possible in the space, the color Red is preferred for decorations, banners, ribbons, etc.

Pentecost was the Jewish festival of Shavuot, or Weeks, which celebrated the harvest fifty days after Passover. On this day, flames appeared over the heads of Jesus' disciples as they preached the Gospel in languages that all could understand. For Christians, this is considered the birthday of the Church. It is a harvest of believers who are brought into the Church universal.

Preparing before the Labyrinth

Sitting or standing, take a moment of quiet contemplation and then read the following:

> The People of Israel celebrated the Harvest, and the Holy
> Spirit came down.
> Like tongues of fire above their heads, the Apostles preached.
> Lead us into the world to Preach the Gospel.
> Guide us in your Way of Love.

Read Psalm 119:105–112:

> Your word is a lamp for my feet,
> a light on my path.
> I have taken an oath and confirmed it,
> that I will follow your righteous laws.
> I have suffered much;
> preserve my life, Lord, according to your word.
> Accept, Lord, the willing praise of my mouth,
> and teach me your laws.
> Though I constantly take my life in my hands,
> I will not forget your law.
> The wicked have set a snare for me,
> but I have not strayed from your precepts.
> Your statutes are my heritage forever;
> they are the joy of my heart.

My heart is set on keeping your decrees
to the very end.

The Labyrinth

Begin the Labyrinth as is most expedient for that space. As you progress through the labyrinth, pray with words about the presence of the Holy Spirit. Alternately, chant to yourself "Come, Holy Spirit, come," as you proceed through your journey.

The Procession from Labyrinth into the World

Holy Spirit, Great Comforter, ignite your holy fire in our hearts; strengthen our faith to share the Gospel in our words, in our thoughts, and in our deeds. Breathe a revival into my heart and into your Church so that we can understand real rejoicing, through Jesus Christ our Lord. *Amen.*

Reflections from the Labyrinth

The Jewish festival of the harvest became the beginning of the blessed harvest of God, wherein people from all across the world found salvation in Jesus. The blood of lambs was replaced with the blood of the Lamb of God. It is the time when we celebrate the great gift that God has given us, the Church, and find peace and hope, love and acceptance, joy and comfort. When we have trouble finding these things, we know to pray and ask God to help re-birth the Church to serve all of God's people.

Questions to ask yourself

- Pentecost is called the birthday of the Church. How can you help rebirth the Church each and every day?

- How do you know when the Holy Spirit is acting through or to you?

- How do you envision the Holy Spirit? Does that matter to you?

A Trinity Sunday Labyrinth Walk

The first Sunday after Pentecost, Trinity Sunday celebrates the doctrine of the Trinity: the Father, the Son, and the Holy Spirit. Traditionally, colorings are to be White if decorating around the Labyrinth.

On Trinity Sunday we read scriptures that refer to God in Three Persons. One of the biggest questions about this Sunday is how we can be monotheists and believe that God consists of three Persons. Even the best minds of history have wrestled with this idea, and most have decided that is where logic may fail and faith reigns supreme.

Preparing before the Labyrinth

Sitting or standing, take a moment of quiet contemplation and then recite:

> We believe in one God,
> the Father, the Almighty,
> maker of heaven and earth,
> of all that is, seen and unseen.
> We believe in one Lord, Jesus Christ,
> the only Son of God,
> eternally begotten of the Father,
> God from God, Light from Light,
> true God from true God,
> begotten, not made,
> of one Being with the Father.
> Through Him all things were made.
> For us and for our salvation
> He came down from heaven:
> by the power of the Holy Spirit
> He became incarnate from the Virgin Mary,
> and was made man.
> For our sake he was crucified under Pontius Pilate;
> he suffered death and was buried.
> On the third day he rose again
> in accordance with the Scriptures;

he ascended into heaven
and is seated at the right hand of the Father.
He will come again in glory to judge the living and the dead,
and his kingdom will have no end.
We believe in the Holy Spirit, the Lord, the giver of life,
who proceeds from the Father and the Son.
With the Father and the Son he is worshiped and glorified.
He has spoken through the Prophets.
We believe in one holy catholic and apostolic Church.
We acknowledge one baptism for the forgiveness of sins.
We look for the resurrection of the dead,
and the life of the world to come. Amen.

The Labyrinth

*Begin the Labyrinth as is most expedient for that space. Any hymn like
"St. Patrick's Breastplate" or others dealing with the Trinity is appropriate. If you don't feel like singing, even to yourself, think about repeating
"Enter my heart and make it pure, Holy Trinity, God in Three Persons
indivisible," or your own terms for the Trinity to yourself.*

The Procession from Labyrinth into the World

Our Father, who art in heaven,
hallowed be thy Name,
thy kingdom come,
thy will be done,
on earth as it is in heaven.
Give us this day our daily bread.
And forgive us our trespasses,
as we forgive those who trespass against us.
And lead us not into temptation,
but deliver us from evil.
For thine is the kingdom, and the power, and the glory,
for ever and ever. Amen.

Holy Trinity, incomprehensible in form and fashion, over-whelming in grace, mercy, and love. We your people praise, worship, and bless you, even when we do not understand. We trust in you, O God. We ask for your presence, protection, and blessings until in that heavenly country we see you face to face and finally understand you fully. *Amen.*

Reflections from the Labyrinth

Of all theological issues in Christianity, the Trinity is one of the most difficult for people to understand. Even those who have studied this doctrine for many years still come to a consensus that it is a mystery. St. Athanasios wrote a personal statement of faith to describe his limited understanding of the Trinity, and it became known as the Athanasian Creed. It is perfectly acceptable to struggle with how the Trinity works and a good and healthy thing to actively wrestle with as a person of faith. Whenever you struggle, remember this: God is God, and he loves you.

Questions to ask yourself

- In your own mind, what does God look like?

- How does God relate to individual people as well as to himself?

- God is One, but in Three Persons of the same substance. How does that make sense in your own mind?

An All Saints' Day Labyrinth Walk

Traditionally, colorings are to be White if decorating around the Labyrinth.

All Saints' Day is a day when we remember those who have gone before us. Even great saints made mistakes. But the good news is that we can learn from their examples. This is helpful as we strive to live better, holier lives and become the best version of ourselves. What kind of saint would we like to be remembered as? Saints are holy and virtuous, and we can learn to become more like them on the labyrinth journey.

Preparing before the Labyrinth

Sitting or standing, take a moment of quiet contemplation and then read Revelation 7:2-4,9-17:

> I saw another angel ascending from the rising of the sun, having the seal of the living God, and he called with a loud voice to the four angels who had been given power to damage earth and sea, saying, "Do not damage the earth or the sea or the trees, until we have marked the servants of our God with a seal on their foreheads." And I heard the number of those who were sealed, one hundred forty-four thousand, sealed out of every tribe of the people of Israel. After this I looked, and there was a great multitude that no one could count, from every nation, from all tribes and peoples and languages, standing before the throne and before the Lamb, robed in white, with palm branches in their hands. They cried out in a loud voice, saying, "Salvation belongs to our God who is seated on the throne, and to the Lamb!" And all the angels stood around the throne and around the elders and the four living creatures, and they fell on their faces before the throne and worshiped God, singing, "Amen! Blessing and glory and wisdom and thanksgiving and honor and power and might be to our God forever and ever! Amen." Then one of the elders addressed me, saying, "Who are these, robed in white, and where have they come from?" I said to him, "Sir, you

are the one that knows." Then he said to me, "These are they who have come out of the great ordeal; they have washed their robes and made them white in the blood of the Lamb."

For this reason they are before the throne of God, and worship Him day and night within His temple, and the one who is seated on the throne will shelter them. They will hunger no more, and thirst no more; the sun will not strike them, nor any scorching heat; for the Lamb at the center of the throne will be their shepherd, and he will guide them to springs of the water of life, and God will wipe away every tear from their eyes."

The Labyrinth

Begin the Labyrinth as is most expedient for that space. It is advisable to sing or listen to hymns about the saints, such as "I sing a song of the saints of God," "For all the saints, who from their labors rest," or "Jerusalem, my happy home." A repetition of "Lord, strengthen me to serve you as did your saints" or "Wash away my fears and strengthen me to do your will, O God" is advised.

The Procession from Labyrinth into the World

Blessed are the poor in spirit,

for theirs is the kingdom of heaven.

Blessed are those who mourn,

for they will be comforted.

Blessed are the meek,

for they will inherit the earth.

Blessed are those who hunger and thirst for righteousness,

for they will be filled.

Blessed are the merciful,

for they will receive mercy.

Blessed are the pure in heart,

for they will see God.

Blessed are the peacemakers,

for they will be called children of God.

Blessed are those who are persecuted for righteousness' sake,
    for theirs is the kingdom of heaven.
Blessed are you when people revile you and persecute you and
    utter all kinds of evil against you falsely on my account.
Rejoice and be glad, for your reward is great in heaven, for in
    the same way they persecuted the prophets who were
    before you.

Reflections from the Labyrinth

We tend to gloss over saints in many churches. Either they are super-human people who are in battle against evil, or they are sad martyrs recovering from their executions. But to be saintly simply means to be holy or virtuous. If we all focus on what keeps us from being truly holy (set aside for God) and virtuous (having high moral standards), we become saints, even if with a lower-case "s." In the labyrinth, we can reflect on what keeps us from sainthood and what helps us approach it.

Questions to ask yourself

- How can I consider myself to be saint-like?

- Where are the issues or attitudes in my life that are preventing me from being more like the saints?

- Were all saints perfect and holy, or did some also have similar issues to mine?

A Christ the King Sunday Labyrinth Walk

Christ the King Sunday celebrates the complete authority of Christ as King and Lord of creation and is the last Sunday before Advent. Traditionally, colorings are to be White if decorating around the Labyrinth.

Christ the King Sunday is a relatively new feast day. It was instituted a hundred years ago to help us remember that our allegiance should be first and foremost to Christ our King.

Preparing before the Labyrinth

Sitting or standing, take a moment of quiet contemplation and then pray:

> O Lord God, King of the Universe, who created and rules all;
> We Praise You and acknowledge you our King.
> O Lord Jesus, through your death and resurrection demonstrated that all powers and dominions, even that of death itself are subject to You, King above all Kings;
> We Praise You and acknowledge You our King.
> O Holy Spirit, whose loving kindness presides over our hearts;
> We Praise You and acknowledge You our King.
> Holy, Triune, indivisible God, You are King of Kings and Lord of Lords, free us from the bonds of sin. Restore in us clean hearts, and show us your mercy in our lives and the lives of all, both those we love and those who we think we hate. Bless our enemies as much as our friends so that we may all come to live under your reign and in your eternal Kingdom forever and ever. *Amen.*

The Labyrinth

Begin the Labyrinth as is most expedient for that space. Try to focus on the meaning of kingdom and Christ being King over all. If you need a prompt, try repeating "My Lord, and my God" to help you focus.

The Procession from Labyrinth into the World

> Our Father, who art in heaven,
> hallowed be thy Name,

thy kingdom come,
thy will be done,
    on earth as it is in heaven.
Give us this day our daily bread.
And forgive us our trespasses,
    as we forgive those who trespass against us.
And lead us not into temptation,
    but deliver us from evil.
For thine is the kingdom, and the power, and the glory,
    for ever and ever. Amen.

King Eternal, Supreme Sovereign, to whom all knees should bend, all heads bow. You have created us, empowered us, and rule over us with loving kindness. We praise You for all you have done and ask your blessings on our lives. May we be good and faithful subjects and citizens of your eternal Kingdom, where with all the saints we may come to rest and worship You forever *Amen.*

Reflections from the Labyrinth

Throughout history, kings often imposed their rule by bloody conquest. But Christ is a different kind of king. He does not force us to submit to his authority; instead, he waits for us to give ourselves freely to his kind and loving rule. Indeed, the ways of heaven are not the broken and fallen ways of earth. Let's focus on this as we ponder the truth of the heavenly kingdom that is referred to in the Lord's Prayer.

ROBERT J. F. ELSNER

Questions to ask yourself

- When you think of God as King, what do you imagine?
- What does God's kingdom really look like?
- If Jesus was physically with you right now in bodily form, how would you really treat him?

∅ 116 ∅

CHAPTER 6

SPECIAL FEAST DAY WALKS

The term "feast" days comes from the Latin word *festes*, which means joy. Some feasts days are dedicated to the lives of special people of faith who inspire us in some ways to better and transform our own lives. While there are feast days for many saints, a few of the most commonly celebrated are included here for contemplation and inspiration.

A Walk for St. Stephen's Day
(Dec. 26)

Traditionally, colorings are to be Red if decorating around the Labyrinth.

Stephen, a deacon and the first Martyr of the Christian faith, is an example of great service, faith, forgiveness, and humility to many. Even as he was being stoned to death, his prayers were to forgive those killing him.

Preparing before the Labyrinth

Sitting or standing, take a moment of quiet contemplation and then read the following scripture and pray:

> Now Stephen, a man full of God's grace and power, performed great wonders and signs among the people. Opposition arose, however, from members of the Synagogue of the Freedmen (as it was called)—Jews of Cyrene and Alexandria as well as the provinces of Cilicia and Asia—who began to argue with Stephen. But they could not stand up against the wisdom the Spirit gave him as he spoke. *(Acts 6:8-10)*

> When the members of the Sanhedrin heard this, they were furious and gnashed their teeth at him. But Stephen, full of the Holy Spirit, looked up to heaven and saw the glory of God, and Jesus standing at the right hand of God. "Look," he said, "I see heaven open and the Son of Man standing at the right hand of God." At this they covered their ears and, yelling at the top of their voices, they all rushed at him, dragged him out of the city and began to stone him. Meanwhile, the witnesses laid their coats at the feet of a young man named Saul. While they were stoning him, Stephen prayed, "Lord Jesus, receive my spirit." Then he fell on his knees and cried out, "Lord, do not hold this sin against them." When he had said this, he fell asleep. *(Acts 7:54-60)*

Jesus, my salvation and strength, I thank you for the example of Stephen, the first Martyr of the Faith. You gave him wisdom and a heart to serve other people. You strengthened him so that instead of cursing those who killed him, he prayed for their forgiveness. From his example many other hearts were turned to you and your love. Breathe into me strength and wisdom, O Lord, and fill my heart with such love that I can serve those in need and truly forgive those who hurt me in any way.

The Labyrinth

Begin the Labyrinth as is most expedient for that space, and if possible, sing or listen to the hymn or similar thematically appropriate music. At the center of the Labyrinth, focus on trust in God and on forgiveness.

> Lord Jesus, receive my spirit. Lord, do not hold their sin against those who hurt me.

The Procession from Labyrinth into the World

God, who received the soul of Stephen and gave him a crown of glory, let me follow his example and serve whomever in need I am able. Help me to be honestly forgiving and strong enough to not bear grudges. Let me see my own faults, fix them, and not compare myself to others except to learn to love You more. *Amen.*

Reflections from the Labyrinth

Many of us fear that when we serve others, we might not receive recognition for our deeds. Yet it is God—and not us—who should be given praise and thanks when we serve others. After all, if we need to hear words of gratitude, we are serving ourselves and looking out for our own self-interests. Stephen is a good example of someone who directed all glory to God. The first martyr to the cause of Christ, he served to advance God's Kingdom and glorify God. By surrendering his life, he became the conduit of God's love. Each of us needs to consider what we do for ourselves, even if we say we are doing it for God. Honesty and charity are key if we wish to honor God.

Questions to ask yourself

- Do you get mad if you help people and they don't say thank you? Why do you get mad?
    - Would that change if you found out that the people later gave their thanks to God in prayer?

- How far would you go to serve God, if your life was endangered by doing what was right?

- Consider: if you say that you will forgive but you will not forget, do you really forgive? Or have you made the statement only for public affirmation?

A Walk for the Feast of the Holy Innocents
(Dec. 28)

Traditionally, colorings are to be Red if decorating around the Labyrinth.

The Holy Innocents are considered martyrs because they were the victims of King Herod's fear and hatred of the child Jesus. Dreading that Jesus would someday take his throne, Herod ordered the death of all baby boys in the land. On this day we focus on love, kindness, and the removal of fear that incites us to do bad things.

Preparing before the Labyrinth

Sitting or standing, take a moment of quiet contemplation and then read this scripture from Matthew 2:16–18 and pray:

Then Herod, when he saw that he was deceived by the wise men, was exceedingly angry; and he sent forth and put to death all the male children who were in Bethlehem and in all its districts, from two years old and under, according to the time which he had determined from the wise men. Then was fulfilled what was spoken by Jeremiah the prophet, saying:

"A voice was heard in Ramah,
Lamentation, weeping, and great mourning,
Rachel weeping for her children,
Refusing to be comforted,
Because they are no more."

Lord, I praise You for your creation, your mercy, and your love. Help me to comprehend that which I do not, especially the loss of life of innocent children. Deliver their souls to your eternal kingdom where they may never know pain or sorrow. Take away the hatred, arrogance, and desperation for control that promotes such evil in this world. Comfort those who have lost children under any circumstances, and let them accept such comfort such that they see your love and mercy in the circumstances and do not become embittered to You and your church. Help us cherish those with us, and remember all the great works You have done. Grow us in faith every day, dear Lord.

The Labyrinth

Begin the Labyrinth as is most expedient for that space, and if desirable, sing or listen to the hymn "What wonderous love is this" or "Jesus loves the little children," or similar thematically appropriate music. At the center of the Labyrinth, focus on seeking God's love in all things, even tragedies.

> Lord, I do not understand, but I trust You. Help me to see what your plan is and realize it in my life.

The Procession from Labyrinth into the World

Great Architect of the Universe, who set the universe in motion and created us to glorify You, I praise you for my life and the lives of those whom I love. Help me and all others to understand the deaths of the innocent, especially children. Whatever the circumstances, enlighten my mind and my heart to your will, your plans, and where we may have erred and strayed from your ways such that events like the Holy Innocents transpire. Embolden me, O Lord, to make whatever changes I can to save life and avoid pain in others, so that all people can come to praise You in wholeness of heart. *Amen.*

Reflections from the Labyrinth

Much evil happens in the world and is often caused by those who are seeking power for themselves at the expense of God's glory. Herod caused the deaths of countless children because of his fear of losing power. Many injustices have been committed against innocents in the cause of power, and it is our job as believers to seek God in all situations, even when we are hurt.

Questions to ask yourself

- Is it always part of God's plan when innocent people die? Why would a just and loving God allow such things to happen?

- Could God not have prevented the murder of so many children and had His purposes accomplished in some other way, or was the evil of men so strong that for a moment they overcame God's purposes?

- When bad things happen to innocent children, do you blame God, or the people who have fallen away from God?

- Where do adversities fit into the development of faith?

A Walk for the Feast of St. Joseph
(Mar. 19)

Traditionally, colorings are to be White if decorating around the Labyrinth.

Joseph is venerated as a holy man who was willing to foster the incarnate God, even if it brought shame and insecurity to him. He sacrificed many things to be the earthly father that Jesus needed.

Preparing before the Labyrinth

Sitting or standing, take a moment of quiet contemplation and then pray after reading Matthew 1:18-20:

> Now the birth of Jesus Christ was on this wise: When as his mother Mary was espoused to Joseph, before they came together, she was found with child of the Holy Ghost. Then Joseph her husband, being a just man, and not willing to make her a public example, was minded to put her away privily. But while he thought on these things, behold, the angel of the Lord appeared unto him in a dream, saying, Joseph, thou son of David, fear not to take unto thee Mary thy wife: for that which is conceived in her is of the Holy Ghost.

I thank you God for the kindness and righteousness of Joseph, that he went against his societal conventions to become an earthly father to our Lord and Savior and a husband to Mary. Help me to be slow to judge and to listen to you and your angels present in my life. Let me see truth and consideration of others now and always.

The Labyrinth

Begin the Labyrinth as is most expedient for that space, and if possible, sing or listen to the hymn "Lord of all Hopefulness" or similar thematically appropriate music. At the center of the Labyrinth, focus on standing up for others, even when it brings inconvenience or ridicule to you.

Strengthen me to be like Joseph, even at the cost of my comfort. Let me stand for what is right.

The Procession from Labyrinth into the World

Lord of all hopefulness, Lord of all joy, thank You for the life and ministry of Joseph. Help me to be so bold and faithful to take on responsibilities that may terrify me but serve your plan for building your Kingdom. Armor me with gentleness and kindness and peace in my heart. *Amen.*

Reflections from the Labyrinth

Joseph was a just and upright man in an era of injustice. He did not break his engagement to Mary, even when he found out that she was pregnant with a child that wasn't his. Instead, he helped the mother and child escape to Egypt when Herod ordered the slaughter of all male babies in Bethlehem. In our lives, it is difficult to know whether we are standing up for God's will and desires or are enabling undesirable behaviors in our society. We do not all have the benefit of angels telling us what to do, but are blessed to have Jesus' commandments and the guidance of the Holy Spirit.

Questions to ask yourself

- How do you decide when to be kind? How do we avoid enabling bad behavior?
- Which matters more when you give a beggar money: What that person does with the gift, or your intentions for giving?
- Would you risk your reputation, and even your life, to do what is right and what you know to be part of God's plan?

A Walk for the Feast of Mary Magdalene
(July 22)

Traditionally, colorings are to be White if decorating around the Labyrinth.

Mary Magdalene was one of the first to follow Jesus, and one of the few to stay with him at the cross. Perhaps most memorable, she is also among those first to whom the Risen Lord appeared. She followed, loved, and supported Jesus in ways that are excellent examples of true faithfulness.

Preparing before the Labyrinth

Sitting or standing, take a moment of quiet contemplation and then pray:

> When Jesus rose early on the first day of the week, he appeared first to Mary Magdalene, out of whom he had driven seven demons. *(Mark 16:9)*

Lord, thank you for the life and example of Mary of Magdala, the first to proclaim Jesus as having risen from the dead. As Mary put all of her trust in Jesus and ministered to him and to the Apostles, teach me to trust in you and to minister to your people as they need. Prepare my heart, O God, to let your love flow through me and bless those around me. Let me not be dismayed, Lord, but overwhelm the world with your mercy.

The Labyrinth

Begin the Labyrinth as is most expedient for that space, and if possible, sing or listen to the hymn or similar thematically appropriate music. At the center of the Labyrinth, focus on this prayer:

> Lord, let me be a servant of truth and mercy. Give me strength for healing others, always trusting in You so that I too am healed.

The Procession from Labyrinth into the World

Savior, Redeemer, and Friend, you comforted Mary, and she comforted you and your Disciples. Comfort me and help me to comfort other people. Stay with me in all times, as Mary stayed with Jesus at the Cross. Open my ears that I may only hear truth about other people, and not utter falsehoods. Open my eyes to see where I might help others and support them. Strengthen my body that I might serve others in whatever ways that truly glorify you. Give me patience such that I see your plans in your time. *Amen.*

Reflections from the Labyrinth

Mary Magdalene, whose surname denotes that she was from the city of Magdala, was an amazing woman, and one of the few people that traveled all over the land with Jesus during his earthly ministry. She was the first person to see the Risen Lord and proclaim his resurrection to the other disciples. She did this from a pure love, not just from gratitude for Jesus curing her of her burden of demons, whatever those were. While scholars argue if she was the same woman who washed Jesus' feet with her tears, it really does not matter. She was one of the few who remained with Jesus, even at the Cross and at the grave.

Questions to ask yourself

- When you read the scriptures, what does it really say about Mary Magdalene? Is this what you thought you knew about her?

- How can you minister to people if you are not given a title (like "Disciple") as others around you are? Does inequality hold you back from serving?

- Do you have the faith to stand up for what you believe like Mary did, even staying with Jesus as he was crucified? How did Mary develop that faith, and how can you follow her example?

A Walk for the Feast of St. Mary the Virgin (Aug. 15)

Traditionally, colorings are to be White if decorating around the Labyrinth.

Mary was a young woman whose faith in God was pure. She offered up her own love and body to serve God fully, even when the world did not understand her sacrifices. Mary knew that the child she bore would be the incarnation of God and that he would die in order to conquer death. She is called the "Theotokos," which means God-bearer, or mother of God.

Preparing before the Labyrinth

Sitting or standing, take a moment of quiet contemplation, read this passage from Luke 1:26-35, and then pray:

> And in the sixth month the angel Gabriel was sent from God unto a city of Galilee, named Nazareth, to a virgin espoused to a man whose name was Joseph, of the house of David; and the virgin's name was Mary. And the angel came in unto her, and said, Hail, thou that art highly favoured, the Lord is with thee: blessed art thou among women. And when she saw him, she was troubled at his saying, and cast in her mind what manner of salutation this should be. And the angel said unto her, Fear not, Mary: for thou hast found favour with God. And, behold, thou shalt conceive in thy womb, and bring forth a son, and shalt call his name JESUS. He shall be great, and shall be called the Son of the Highest: and the Lord God shall give unto him the throne of his father David: And he shall reign over the house of Jacob for ever; and of his kingdom there shall be no end. Then said Mary unto the angel, How shall this be, seeing I know not a man? And the angel answered and said unto her, The Holy Ghost shall come upon thee, and the power of the Highest shall overshadow thee: therefore also that holy thing which shall be born of thee shall be called the Son of God.

I thank You, dearest Lord, for the life and faith of Mary. Although young, she followed her faith despite societal pressures that she knew would condemn her. She risked all for You and your plan of salvation for the world. I beg that You grant me such strength of conviction and such awareness of the world that I may not be bitter at the load you give me to bear. Strengthen me for service, Lord, and grant me the resolve to carry through all my tasks of love. *Amen.*

The Labyrinth

Begin the Labyrinth as is most expedient for that space, and if possible, sing or listen to the hymn "Blest are the pure in heart" or "Ave Maria" or "Salve Regina" or similar thematically appropriate music. At the center of the Labyrinth, focus on

Take my life, Lord, to fulfill your purposes. Enrobe me with faith and love, and never let me falter.

The Procession from Labyrinth into the World

And Mary said, My soul doth magnify the Lord, and my spirit hath rejoiced in God my Saviour. For He hath regarded the low estate of His handmaiden: for, behold, from henceforth all generations shall call me blessed. For He that is mighty hath done to me great things; and holy is His name. And His mercy is on them that fear Him from generation to generation. He hath shewed strength with His arm; He hath scattered the proud in the imagination of their hearts. He hath put down the mighty from their seats, and exalted them of low degree. He hath filled the hungry with good things; and the rich He hath sent empty away. He hath holpen his servant Israel, in remembrance of His mercy; As He spake to our fathers, to Abraham, and to His seed for ever. And Mary abode with her about three months, and returned to her own house. *(Luke 1:46-51)*

I praise you, Ruler of Heaven, for the life and example of Mary, mother of God. Through her strength of faith, she was able to bear and raise our Lord, caring for him and ministering to him in his times of need. Help me to have the faith and resolve of Mary, so that I too may follow and serve. Take away my fears and doubts, even if you do not send angels to reassure me. *Amen.*

Reflections from the Labyrinth

Mary had a depth of faith that most people cannot comprehend. She was a girl about to become a young woman, and she was given the weighty task of bearing God incarnate. Even though she knew she would face ridicule and possibly even be stoned to death for following God's plan for her, she still obeyed. The name she gave her baby, Yeshua, Hebrew for "Salvation," is a testament to her unyielding faith that her child would save Israel, as is her courage to flee to Egypt to avoid Herod's murderous rage.

Though her name means "bitter," and she had every right to be resentful of God's plan for her, Mary never hesitated to follow through with God's plan. She stayed with her son at the risk of her life, even at the foot of the cross, and then continued to follow him until he ascended. She was truly a picture of faithfulness and a model for how we are supposed to act as true and faithful followers of God.

Questions to ask yourself

- How can you develop your faith to be completely trusting, as Mary was? What holds you back from such faith?
- How can you face so many trials and tribulations and not become bitter towards God or towards people?
- Would you be able to forgive those who ridiculed you or chased you from your home as Mary did?
- Where in our lives do we carry Jesus and care for him?

A Walk for the Feast of St. Michael and All Angels
(Sept. 29)

Traditionally, colorings are to be White if decorating around the Labyrinth.

Michael, chief archangel, was the leader of the armies of Heaven who defeated Satan in battle. His name poses a challenge, literally translating to "Who is like God?" and inspires us to seek out God and understand Him better. Michael and all of the angels love and serve God with their entire being and help us to continually seek out God and a closer walk with our Risen Lord.

Preparing before the Labyrinth

Sitting or standing, take a moment of quiet contemplation, read Psalm 103:19-22, and then pray:

> The LORD has set His throne in heaven, * and His kingship has dominion over all.
> Bless the LORD, you angels of His, you mighty ones who do His bidding, * and hearken to the voice of His word.
> Bless the LORD, all you His hosts, * you ministers of His who do His will.
> Bless the LORD, all you works of His, in all places of His dominion; * bless the LORD, O my soul.

Everlasting God, who created all things, thank you for the angels who minister to me and to us all, whether I understand it or not. As angels ministered to Jesus in the wilderness and brought our forebearers messages of peace and of warning, please send your angels to minister to my fears and doubts that I might fully honor you with my life. I praise you for the existence of Michael and other angels who I know do battle against the forces of evil and ask to be strengthened to combat all sin that separates me from you. *Amen.*

The Labyrinth

Begin the Labyrinth as is most expedient for that space, and if possible, sing or listen to the hymn "Holy God we Praise Thy Name" or similar thematically appropriate music. At the center of the Labyrinth, focus on the messages for which angels are known.

Open my mind, Lord, to hear the messages You send. Grant angelic protection over me.

The Procession from Labyrinth into the World

I saw the Lord seated on a throne, high and exalted; and the train of His robe filled the temple. Above Him stood seraphim, each having six wings: With two wings they covered their faces, with two they covered their feet, and with two they were flying. And they were calling out to one another:

"Holy, holy, holy is the LORD of Hosts;
all the earth is full of His glory."

At the sound of their voices the doorposts and thresholds shook, and the temple was filled with smoke. *(Isaiah 6:1-4)*

Glory to You, Creator of all things, judge of all people, who made angels to be messengers to humanity. Angels spoke with Jacob and Abraham, with Joshua and with the Disciples. Angels worship You day and night, while we should be doing the same. I thank You for the angels and the reminders of your love and protection to save us, so often from ourselves and our lack of faith. As the Archangel Michael leads the heavenly host in battle against evil, so empower me to fight off the snares and traps of evil in all its forms here on earth. Help me be an angel of mercy and kindness here on earth, spreading the good news of salvation and hope to all people. *Amen.*

Reflections from the Labyrinth

Most of us think of angels as being the beautiful, bird-winged people from renaissance art. Of course, what they look like does not really matter; their function does. Angels are God's messengers—warriors and agents who assist humanity. Angels are not there to get us out of every scrape, but to help guide and teach us. It is up to us to follow their guidance and learn to be like them. Like angels, we are here in this world to proclaim, "Holy, Holy, Holy!"

Questions to ask yourself

- Who has worked for God in being an angel in your life, bringing messages of hope, love, or admonition?

- While we have ideas of things like "guardian angels," do we need a personal angel to watch over us, or do we need to help do that for each other?

- When do you act as God's messenger, and when are you afraid or embarrassed to share the Gospel?

- When are you unwilling to help others and get involved?

A Walk for the Feast of St. James of Jerusalem (Oct. 23)

Traditionally, colorings are to be Red if decorating around the Labyrinth.

James, one of the disciples, was the first Bishop of Jerusalem. He was martyred because of his unyielding faith in God.

Preparing before the Labyrinth

Sitting or standing, take a moment of quiet contemplation, read this passage from the Epistle of James 1:19-27, and then pray:

> Wherefore, my beloved brethren, let every man be swift to hear, slow to speak, slow to wrath: For the wrath of man worketh not the righteousness of God. Wherefore lay apart all filthiness and superfluity of naughtiness, and receive with meekness the engrafted word, which is able to save your souls. But be ye doers of the word, and not hearers only, deceiving your own selves. For if any be a hearer of the word, and not a doer, he is like unto a man beholding his natural face in a glass: For he beholdeth himself, and goeth his way, and straightway forgetteth what manner of man he was. But whoso looketh into the perfect law of liberty, and continueth therein, he being not a forgetful hearer, but a doer of the work, this man shall be blessed in his deed. If any man among you seem to be religious, and bridleth not his tongue, but deceiveth his own heart, this man's religion is vain. Pure religion and undefiled before God and the Father is this, To visit the fatherless and widows in their affliction, and to keep himself unspotted from the world.

Lord, thank You for the work of James, first Bishop of Jerusalem. His life and teachings help us grow to be honest and good, truly doers of the Word, not just hearers. Help us to hear and do your Word and Commandments in our lives. Guard our tongues so that the words we speak may be sweet and pure, always to your glory and the benefit to all your creation. *Amen.*

The Labyrinth

Begin the Labyrinth as is most expedient for that space, and if possible, sing or listen to the hymn "By all your Saints Still Striving" or similar thematically appropriate music. At the center of the Labyrinth, focus on doing, not just hearing the Gospel.

Help me to do the works You have given me, O God, not simply hearing them. Write your laws in my heart and make my actions true.

The Procession from Labyrinth into the World

Who is wise and understanding among you? Let him show it by his good conduct, by deeds done in the humility that comes from wisdom. But if you harbor bitter jealousy and selfish ambition in your hearts, do not boast in it or deny the truth. Such wisdom does not come from above, but is earthly, unspiritual, demonic. For where jealousy and selfish ambition exist, there will be disorder and every evil practice. But the wisdom from above is first of all pure, then peace-loving, gentle, accommodating, full of mercy and good fruit, impartial, and sincere. Peacemakers who sow in peace reap the fruit of righteousness. (*James 3:13–18*)

Thank you, Lord, for the life and work of the Apostle James. Help me to do all you have given me to do and to be humble and honest throughout my life and interactions with myself and others. Give me a pure heart that can honestly be content and yet willing to work for your purposes. Guide me to avoid evil and arrogance, and stand for truth, even in spite of risks. *Amen.*

Reflections from the Labyrinth

James was a beloved disciple who went with Jesus everywhere and served as the first Bishop of Jerusalem. He was martyred for his faith when he was beaten to death and thrown off the pinnacle of the Temple. Though he suffered such a gruesome end, James serves as an example of the risks of being honest and true. There is an old bumper sticker from the 1970s that asked: "If you were accused of being a Christian, would there be enough evidence to convict you?" James risked his life to be a peacemaker and speak truth with kindness. His faithfulness was a source of distress among others but was the right course of action.

Questions to ask yourself

- Do you really try to live the Christian life, or do you simply wear the label?

- What does it look like to overcome natural ambition and serve God and humanity?

- Have you ever focused on what your ambitions are, and where they might not be in line with God's plans for you?

- Do you have to tell people that you are a Christian, or do they see it in the overwhelming love and kindness you show, even while admonishing?

CHAPTER 7

SPECIAL OCCASION WALKS

There are occasions where the labyrinth can provide a special venue for contemplative worship, either alone or with another person. The following Walks are to serve in this capacity, focusing on Healing, Reconciliation, Liberation, and Justice. While there are liturgies for some of these issues, there is also a need for individuals to completely focus on them and integrate the ideas of peace and wellness into themselves.

A Healing Walk in the Labyrinth

As this experience is outside of ecclesiastical tradition, colorings should be White if decorating around the Labyrinth.

    Healing is an important part of the Church, and many services exist for regular church worship and healing. This Walk may be done alone or with another person. If a friend or minister is with you, holding hands, linking arms, or other contact is advised, if possible. Minister to each other in Presence.

Preparing before the Labyrinth

Sitting or standing, take a moment of quiet contemplation and then pray:

> O Lord God, King of the Universe, who set the stars and
>   planets in their courses;
> We Praise You and bless your creation.
> O Holy Spirit, who moved over the face of the waters and
>   caused life to begin;
> We Praise You and bless your creation.
> O Father of us all, who formed us from clay and breathed life
>   into us;
> We Praise You and bless your creation.
> O Jesus, who caused the blind to see, the lame to walk, and the
>   dead to be restored;
> We Praise You and bless your creation.
> Holy God, Lover of souls, we ask for healing in mind, body,
>   and soul;
> We Praise You and bless your creation.
> Look upon all your children, O God;
> Who put their trust in You.
> Lay your healing hand upon us;
> Say the word and we shall be healed.

> Lord, our paths are not straight and wide, but curved and narrow. Guide us to You and your healing presence, Dearest Lord. Let us feel your grace and power in healing, as the woman at the

synagogue[1], let us no longer be bent over in pain, but stand and praise God.

The Labyrinth

The Labyrinth courses may be traveled in silence or in singing of a chant, such as "Ubi Caritas."

> *If alone, please use this prayer at the center of the labyrinth:*

O Great Physician, Bless me, your beloved child. Heal me of pain, suffering, and confusion. Strengthen me for your service in faith and focus. I ask this in the Name of the Father, Son, and Holy Spirit. Amen.

If with another person, please consider this form: A foot washing is appropriate if you are walking the Labyrinth with others. You should begin the Labyrinth as is most expedient for that space. At the center of the Labyrinth, if present, the Minister should lay hands on the person in need as they arrive at the center, saying:

O Great Physician, Bless this, your beloved child. Heal her/him of pain, suffering, and confusion. Strengthen her/him for your service in faith and focus. I ask this in the Name of the Father, Son, and Holy Spirit. Amen.

The Labyrinth courses may be traveled in silence or in singing of a chant, such as "Ubi Caritas."

The Procession from Labyrinth into the World

Our Father, who art in heaven,
> hallowed be thy Name,
> thy kingdom come,
> thy will be done,
>> on earth as it is in heaven.
Give us this day our daily bread.
And forgive us our trespasses,

---

1. Luke 13:13

as we forgive those who trespass against us.
And lead us not into temptation,
    but deliver us from evil.
For thine is the kingdom, and the power, and the glory,
    for ever and ever. Amen.

Almighty and loving God, who knows all the hairs on our heads and all stars in the heavens, I thank You for the centering of my heart and mind on You, your mercy, and your love for all of us. I beg your mercy that my path may be simple and wide, with no stumbling blocks before me. Heal my brokenness where I am afflicted in mind, body, or spirit. Pour out your love and healing upon me and those I love now and always. Have mercy on me, beloved Lord, through Jesus Christ, who with You and the Holy Ghost, be all honor and glory, world without end. *Amen.*

Reflections from the Labyrinth

Healing takes many forms. Not all forms of healing are visible, and not all are immediate. As you pray for healing, whether in mind, body, or spirit, give thanks! What are you thankful for, even while being hurt or broken? Who has entered your life and your heart and helped you in this time of travail? Seeking to worship God while asking for healing is a great step to finding restoration and renewal in unexpected ways.

Questions to ask yourself

- In your labyrinth journey, did you thank God for the blessings you have, even when afflicted with pain?

- When should healing occur for the particular issue or illness for which you prayed on this walk? Is healing always what and how we expect it to be? What if God's plans are different and much better than we can imagine?

• Which is more important to be healed: body or spirit? Are you (or any of us) aware of which is which?

A Walk of Reconciliation in the Labyrinth

While outside of ecclesiastical traditions, the suggested colorings should be White if decorating around the Labyrinth.

One of the most needed activities in the world has always been reconciliation. Since Cain and Abel, humans have divided and fought, and are not always able to come back together. Even if you cannot think of a person you need to reconcile with, there is an opportunity here to pray for reconciliation between all of God's children.

Preparing before the Labyrinth

Sitting or standing, take a moment of quiet contemplation and then pray:

O God, who has blessed us with rational minds and loving hearts, help me to focus on You. As a Child of Adam and Eve, I know that I am Fallen. I beg You, O God, to forgive me so that I may be reconciled to other people and to You. Fill my hearts with your peace. Remind me always of the words Christ taught us: Forgive us our trespasses as we forgive those who trespass against us. For if we do not forgive one another, neither will You forgive us. Let me always submit to your will, walk in your ways, and love other people as You love us: in Holiness, Peace, and Forgiveness. Help me to reconcile with those with whom I am out of good and wholesome relationship. Help me to reconcile with others so that I might participate in the communion of souls that is our faith.

> Out of the depths I cry to You, Lord;
> Lord, hear my voice.
> Let your ears be attentive
> to my cry for mercy.
> If You, Lord, kept a record of sins,
> Lord, who could stand?
> But with You there is forgiveness,
> so that we can, with reverence, serve You.
> I wait for the Lord, my whole being waits,
> and in His word I put my hope.

I wait for the Lord
more than watchmen wait for the morning,
more than watchmen wait for the morning.
Israel, put your hope in the Lord,
for with the Lord is unfailing love
and with Him is full redemption.
He Himself will redeem Israel
from all their sins. *(Psalm 130)*

Lord Jesus, your Blessed Cross is a symbol of our brokenness
and sin. I ask your guidance and peace that I may be reconciled
to you, to all those whom I have had problems or offended, and
to all your creation. Let me take up the cross and follow you as
Simon of Cyrene did, helping you to complete your purposes
on this earth. Like Simon, I am a stranger to your Kingdom.
Like Simon, I can only carry the cross for a short time, and
I know that I do not suffer the crucifixion that redeemed me.
Let me suffer for you only to learn to release all that I carry
to your final care that my lives may truly be dedicated to you
in Love.

*A palm or a cross (wood, paper, folded palm, or other) should be held or
carried while journeying through the labyrinth.*

The Labyrinth

*Begin the Labyrinth as is most expedient for that space, and if possible,
sing or listen to the hymn "Amazing Grace" or similar thematically appropriate music. While journeying the Labyrinth, focus on what relationships
need to be reconciled, whether with those alive, those who have passed on,
or those yet to come. At the center of the labyrinth, whether you are journeying on foot or following along with your finger on a paper labyrinth,
lay down that cross you've been carrying and pray:*

In Mark's Gospel, he tells us that "they compelled a passerby,
Simon of Cyrene, who was coming in from the country, the
father of Alexander and Rufus, to carry his cross." Help me, O

Lord, to carry your cross when you ask, and to understand why I might be compelled with the burden. Help me, God, to know that I am not you and am not the one who was crucified for my own sins. *Amen*

In the name of our Blessed Redeemer, I ask to put down the cross that I bear, knowingly or unknowingly. Let the burden of contention cease within me and between me and all people. Let me be at peace and love others as Christ loves me. Let me learn to love myself so that there is no room in my heart for disagreement or arrogance.

The Procession from Labyrinth into the World

Our Father, who art in heaven,
> hallowed be thy Name,
> thy kingdom come,
> thy will be done,
>> on earth as it is in heaven.

Give us this day our daily bread.
And forgive us our trespasses,
> as we forgive those who trespass against us.

And lead us not into temptation,
> but deliver us from evil.

For thine is the kingdom, and the power, and the glory,
> for ever and ever. Amen.

Forgive me, God, for what I have done and left undone that has caused breaks in relationships with others, for sins known and unknown that burden my heart. Tear down all walls that separate me from others or cause me to be defensive or arrogant, so that I may serve you in wholeness of being. Help me to hear and feel what has been described as the peace of God, which passes all understanding. Please let it keep my heart and mind focused on the knowledge and love of You, on the mercy and compassion of Jesus Christ, and the guidance and fellowship of the Holy Spirit. I ask that the blessing of

God Almighty, the Father, the Son, and the Holy Ghost, be on me, and remain with me always. *Amen.*

Reflections from the Labyrinth

Most of us have broken relationships in our lives, whether through our own fault or the fault of others. We do not always recognize when we have broken those relationships through negligence or offhand comments that hurt others more deeply than we imagined. Jesus was an example of reconciliation, always trying to offer forgiveness and healing, seeking out peace and love, even if he had to bring people back from the dead to complete the reconciling process. Through prayers of healing and wholeness we come to terms with our losses and open doors for reconciliation.

Questions to ask yourself

- If you think about relationships that have gone wrong in your life, even if it was obviously the other person's fault, where could you have changed the course and nature of the relationship to bring about reconciliation?

- Who is responsible for the beginning of reconciliation?

- When, if ever, is it better to not reconcile with someone?

A Walk for Liberation

While this is outside of ecclesiastical traditions, colorings should be White if decorating around the Labyrinth.

Liberation can be freedom from oppression, enslavement, human trafficking, addiction, abuse, or many other horrors in life. While many of us cannot understand slavery as described in scripture or in human history, it still exists in many forms today.

Preparing before the Labyrinth

Sitting or standing, take a moment of quiet contemplation and then pray, beginning with this reading from Luke, Chapter 4:

[16] He went to Nazareth, where he had been brought up, and on the Sabbath day he went into the synagogue, as was his custom. He stood up to read, [17] and the scroll of the prophet Isaiah was handed to him. Unrolling it, he found the place where it is written:

[18] "The Spirit of the Lord is on me,
because he has anointed me
to proclaim good news to the poor.
He has sent me to proclaim freedom for the prisoners
and recovery of sight for the blind,
to set the oppressed free,
[19] to proclaim the year of the Lord's favor."

[20] Then he rolled up the scroll, gave it back to the attendant and sat down. The eyes of everyone in the synagogue were fastened on him. [21] He began by saying to them, "Today this scripture is fulfilled in your hearing."

O Author of Freedom, by whose might and mercy we are free, look on your creation with compassion. Help me to remember all who are not free, in body, mind, or spirit. Break the chains of oppression of all types, especially those which I cannot understand. Empower me to love and serve you and all of your people. Awaken my eyes to see your mercy and truth in all things, all situations, and all people. Give me patience, O Lord, but also give me the strength to work for your purposes, freeing myself and others where we are not free. Remind me each day that you are the source of all freedom. "It is for freedom that Christ has set us free. Stand firm, then, and do not let yourselves be burdened again by a yoke of slavery." *(Galatians 5:1)*

The Labyrinth

Begin the Labyrinth as is most expedient for that space, and if possible, sing or listen to the hymn "There's a Wideness in God's Mercy," "O for a thousand tongues to sing," or a similar thematically appropriate music. At the center of the Labyrinth, focus on what freedom means to you, for yourself and for others. If you cannot find words to pray, repeat something like this:

> Lord, help me understand what freedom is, giving myself to You and You alone. Help me to act where I can to free others, that they may find and love You.

The Procession from Labyrinth into the World

Now the Lord is the Spirit, and where the Spirit of the Lord is, there is freedom. *(2 Corinthians 3:17, NIV)*. Lord, pour into me knowledge and understanding of freedom. Help me to see freedom as more than simply not wearing chains or the ability to move around. Remind me, Lord, that there are forms of freedom I may not understand, and types of slavery I cannot know. Empower me, Beloved God, to act as an instrument of freedom, helping me to deliver others from their bonds where I can. Give my sympathy and empathy for others, freeing me from arrogance, embracing me further with your love. *Amen.*

Reflections from the Labyrinth

For many of us, we think of freedom in simple terms. We might think of slavery and indentured servitude as a lack of freedom. We might think of those incarcerated as not having freedom. Yet, freedom is more than this. Some people do not have freedom because they are stuck in bad relationships, enduring economic hardship, or confined by physical disabilities. While some of these challenges can be overcome, others cannot. The most virulent forms of oppression are those of mind and of soul. Psalm 119 tells us that: "I will walk about in freedom, for I have sought out your precepts." This reminds us that the commandments that God gave us are not to bind us, but to set us free, including from ourselves and our selfishness.

Questions to ask yourself

- Where does lack of faith in God bind you?

- How does arrogance directly hurt you and your relationships with God and with other people?

- What forms of oppression and bondage might you not recognize in other people around you as being a loss of their full freedom to be who God intended them to be?

- Where and how might the slavery to sin be broken. For you and for those you love?

- How can you open a discussion with people about what is really binding them from perfect freedom in God's love and mercy?

A Walk for Justice

While this is beyond out church traditions, colorings should be White if decorating around the Labyrinth.

Justice is a familiar theme in scripture, and a major concern for our modern lives. Whether it is in our power to make a more just world or not, it helps to pray for and consider justice in our lives and the lives of others.

Preparing before the Labyrinth

Sitting or standing, take a moment of quiet contemplation and then pray:

> Seek the LORD and live,
> lest he break out like fire in the house of Joseph,
>> and it devour, with none to quench it for Bethel,
> O you who turn justice to wormwood
>> and cast down righteousness to the earth!
> But let justice roll down like waters
>> and righteousness like an ever-flowing stream.
> *(Amos 5:6–7, 24)*

Cloak me in a love of justice, O God, and empower me to stand up for those who cannot stand up for themselves. Let all forms of justice wash over me and clean me from all selfishness, jealousy, or ill intent that may taint my soul. Let my thirst for justice be true, not simply to diminish irritation of others:

> And he told them a parable to the effect that they ought always to pray and not lose heart. He said, "In a certain city there was a judge who neither feared God nor respected man. And there was a widow in that city who kept coming to him and saying, 'Give me justice against my adversary.' For a while he refused, but afterward he said to himself, 'Though I neither fear God nor respect man, yet because this widow keeps bothering me, I will give her justice, so that she will not beat me down by

her continual coming.'" And the Lord said, "Hear what the unrighteous judge says. And will not God give justice to His elect, who cry to him day and night? Will he delay long over them? I tell you, he will give justice to them speedily. Nevertheless, when the Son of Man comes, will he find faith on earth?" *(Luke 18:1–8)*

Build my faith, O God. Help me to believe and trust in you more and more each day.

A palm, stone, or wooden cross could be carried through the labyrinth as a reminder of the burden of justice. If you carry such a burden, leave it at the center of the labyrinth.

The Labyrinth

Begin the Labyrinth as is most expedient for that space, and if possible, sing or listen to the hymn or similar thematically appropriate music. At the center of the Labyrinth, focus on being truly just and equitable to all people, honoring God's commands to us all. Alternately, read and reread the following scripture to help you pray:

Thus says the LORD: Do justice and righteousness, and deliver from the hand of the oppressor him who has been robbed. And do no wrong or violence to the resident alien, the fatherless, and the widow, nor shed innocent blood in this place. *(Jeremiah 22:3)*

The Procession from Labyrinth into the World

Our Father, who art in heaven,
   hallowed be thy Name,
   thy kingdom come,
   thy will be done,
      on earth as it is in heaven.
Give us this day our daily bread.
And forgive us our trespasses,

as we forgive those who trespass against us.
And lead us not into temptation,
but deliver us from evil.
For thine is the kingdom, and the power, and the glory,
for ever and ever. Amen.

Judge Supreme, who is the final authority on all things, cleanse my heart and mind of any inclination to be unjust, bitter, or vindictive. Declare me innocent of all evil and hatred so that I might become pure. In your great wisdom and compassion, make me serve your Kingdom and build that City of Peace where all your children are loved and injustice cannot enter. *Amen.*

Reflections from the Labyrinth

Justice tends to be categorized into four big groupings: distributive (deciding who gets what), procedural (determining how to treat people fairly for the circumstances), retributive (punishment for wrong-doing), and restorative (restoring relationships and healing). There are other forms based on these, such as social justice, environmental justice, economic justice, etc., but they fall in those four main categories. All forms of justice are part of the Church, and all are important to God. Each and every person has a role to play in making this a just world and building the Kingdom of God "on earth **as** it is in heaven." Through prayer and opening our hearts to God, we can truly consider justice from other people's perspectives, even if they are very different from our own.

Questions to ask yourself

* When you think of the word "justice," what is the first thing that comes to mind?

- What are the injustices that make you mad, and what are the injustices that other people care about but you really don't?

- What was the last injustice that you heard/read about that you dismissed as silly or not really an injustice? Why might you think that?

A Mother's Day Walk in the Labyrinth
(second Sunday of May)

Traditionally, colorings are to be White if decorating around the Labyrinth.

Mother's Day celebrates the influence of mothers and other mother figures in society and the irreplaceable role they play in the family unit. This day serves to honor their unconditional love and sacrifice.

Preparing before the Labyrinth

Sitting or standing, take a moment of quiet contemplation and then pray:

O Lord God, who protects us like a mother hen and cares for our every need, I thank You for those who have mothered to me. Help me to cherish the mothers in my life and in the lives around me.

"Your mother was like a vine in a vineyard planted beside the waters; she bore lush fruit and foliage because of the plentiful water, and she produced mighty branches, fit for rulers' scepters." *Ezekiel 19:10–11*

"When a woman gives birth, she has pain because her time has come. But when the child is born, she no longer remembers her distress because of her joy that a child has been born into the world." *John 16:21*

Jerusalem, Jerusalem, you who kill the prophets and stone those sent to you, how often I have longed to gather your children together, as a hen gathers her chicks under her wings, and you were not willing. Look, your house is left to you desolate. *Matthew 23:37–38*

The Labyrinth

Begin the Labyrinth as is most expedient for that space. At the center of the Labyrinth, or during the whole journey, consider repeating:

O God who bore us and gave us life, bless all mothers and those who act as mothers to us, your children. *Amen.*

The Procession from Labyrinth into the World

> O God, author of life. You are Father and Mother and Brother
> to us. Look with compassion on all mothers. Strengthen those
> who struggle with any parts or facets of mothering. Gladden the
> hearts of mothers that they may cause other hearts to be eter-
> nally loving and hopeful. Heal those who wanted to be mothers
> but could not for whatever reason. Guide those who are moth-
> ering such that their children flourish. *Amen.*

Reflections from the Labyrinth

Mothers are some of the most important people in our lives. But,
not all of us have great relationships with our mothers or are good
at mothering ourselves. Luckily, God has provided us with love and
nourishment, wrapped us in warmth and safety, and given us all that
we need, whether we recognize that or not. On Mother's Day, it is
important for us to ponder the maternal love of God and remember
all of those who have mothered us and lived in His image.

Questions to ask yourself

- What are the ways that your mother showed forth as an image
  of God in any way?

- How can you recognize the importance of the various forms of
  motherhood around you?

- Can a man show the spirit of mothering described in scripture?
  Does society allow that?

CHAPTER 8

SPECIAL PUBLIC HOLIDAY WALKS

There are times when we celebrate holidays outside of the Church during which we still need to focus on our relationships, not just with God but with others in our world. The following Walks are intended to serve as examples for some of these holidays.

A Walk for Dr. Martin Luther King, Jr. Day
(Third Monday in January)

Traditionally, colorings are to be Red if decorating around the Labyrinth.

The Reverend Dr. Martin Luther King, Jr. was a leader of the Civil Rights Movement. He is honored throughout the world as a champion of human rights and non-violent protest. In the Church, he is honored for reminding us to study scripture and to adjust our behaviors to align with God's commandments.

Preparing before the Labyrinth

Sitting or standing, take a moment of quiet contemplation and then pray:

King of Heaven, in whose all-loving and faithful image we were all created, help us to see You in all our fellow travelers through this life. Thank You, our only Master, for the life and work of Dr. Martin Luther King, Jr. and all others who have worked and struggled and gave their lives for the cause of freedom. Help me to feel and honor the sacrifice of those whose names are lost to history and who fought for justice.

> O God, You made us in your own image and redeemed us through Jesus your Son: Look with compassion on the whole human family; take away the arrogance and hatred which infect our hearts; break down the walls that separate us; unite us in bonds of love; and work through our struggle and confusion to accomplish your purposes on earth; that, in your good time, all nations and races may serve you in harmony around your heavenly throne; through Jesus Christ our Lord. *Amen.*[1]

The Labyrinth

Begin the Labyrinth as is most expedient for that space, and if you feel comfortable, sing or listen to the hymn "There Is a Balm in Gilead," "Rock

---

1. BCP, p. 815

*of Ages," or similar thematically appropriate music. During the labyrinth
journey, consider a repeated prayer such as:*

> The sacrifices of God are a broken spirit: a broken and a con-
> trite heart, O God, thou wilt not despise. *(Psalm 51:17)*

> Give me strength to love and forgive. Remove from me all thirst
> for vengeance, replaced by a hunger for forgiveness and peace.
> Let me love beyond measure and seek justice and unity beyond
> hope.

*At the center of the Labyrinth, try not to focus on the times when you
may have felt oppressed or belittled. Instead, focus on the times in your life
where you may have oppressed, belittled, or dismissed the personhood of
another child of God, asking God for forgiveness and remembering God's
loving mercy.*

The Procession from Labyrinth into the World

Creator of all, in whose image we are all made from the same
clay and dust, I thank You for the life and example of Dr. Martin
Luther King, Jr. and all others who have fought the good fight
for unity, peace, and equality. Grant that in my heart I may grow
to love all your creation, and show dignity and respect to all people, especially those with whom I disagree or have hard feelings
towards. Help me to stand up for justice, even when it is uncomfortable and may be risky. Let us see from the mountaintop the
wonders of your beloved world and strive to build your kingdom.
Amen.

Reflections from the Labyrinth

In one of his most famous speeches, Dr. King said:

> I have a dream that one day this nation will rise up and live
> out the true meaning of its creed. We hold these truths to be
> self-evident that all men are created equal.
>
> I have a dream that one day out in the red hills of Georgia
> the sons of former slaves and the sons of former slaveowners
> will be able to sit down together at the table of brotherhood.[2]

As a people, we should ponder what it means to be created equal
and have inalienable rights. Contemplate how we can follow the
mandates Jesus gave to us: "Go therefore and make disciples of all
nations, baptizing them in the name of the Father and of the Son
and of the Holy Spirit" *(Matthew 28:19, NRSV)*, and "Go ye into all
the world, and preach the gospel" *(Mark 16:15, KJV)*.

Questions to ask yourself

- How do I avoid contributing to the oppression of other people?
- Where do my biases and bigotries come from? Do I feel them, or
  am I simply repeating what I have heard for so long?
- What does it mean to "Go … and preach the gospel"?
- How can I see other people as fellow children of God, not simply
  as "other"?

---

2. Video and transcript available at: https://www.marshall.edu/onemarshallu/i-have-a-dream/

A Walk for Juneteenth
(June 19th)

Another event outside of Church tradition, colorings should be White if decorating around the Labyrinth.

On June 19th, 1865, Union troops arrived in Galveston Bay, Texas. There they made an astonishing announcement to enslaved peoples: Two years earlier, President Lincoln proclaimed their freedom in the Emancipation Proclamation. This celebration commemorates that fateful day and can help us celebrate the freedom we all enjoy under the Kingship of God.

Preparing before the Labyrinth

Sitting or standing, take a moment of quiet contemplation and then pray:

> ¹⁵And how shall they preach, except they be sent? as it is written, How beautiful are the feet of them that preach the gospel of peace, and bring glad tidings of good things! *(Romans 10:15)*

O Lord God, from whom all gracious blessings flow, I praise You for information and knowledge that sets us free. Thank You for the messengers who strove to carry the good news of liberty to those enslaved. Continue to send forth your angels from heaven and on earth as messengers of your love, whereby we are all continually set free from all forms of oppression and slavery, including those into which we enslave ourselves.

The Labyrinth

Begin the Labyrinth as is most expedient for that space. If you feel comfortable, sing or listen to the hymn "Lift Every Voice and Sing" or similar thematically appropriate music. As you proceed, try to pray something like this:

> Set your people free, O God. Help me to earnestly pray for those who have oppressed me or those whom I love. Make me a blessing to the lives of those who hate or misunderstand me.

At the center of the Labyrinth, focus on ways that you can forgive people who have made you feel that your value was diminished, then meditate on those thoughts and begin your journey toward forgiveness.

The Procession from Labyrinth into the World

Lord, I am your image-bearer. Give me the strength to make peace and forgive others. Grant me mercy and patience, tempered with the ability to act when needed to serve all your people. Remove any and all traces of hatred or bias from me. Remind me each day that You love us all and that we are equal in your sight. *Amen.*

Reflections from the Labyrinth

Juneteenth celebrates the news of freedom that reached the last enslaved people in the United States. In Matthew 5:43-44, Jesus tells us: "Ye have heard that it hath been said, Thou shalt love thy neighbor, and hate thine enemy. But I say unto you, Love your enemies, bless them that curse you, do good to them that hate you, and pray for them which despitefully use you, and persecute you." This is very difficult in our daily lives, especially when some people are actively sowing seeds of racism, sexism, homophobia, or any other form of oppression that dehumanizes God's children. As you reflect on the labyrinth journey, consider deeply how can you be more Christ-like in thought and action.

Questions to ask yourself

- What does oppression look like in the lives of people around me?
- What are the sins that provide the worst oppression in my life, whether I acknowledge them or not?

- What does it really look like to pray for our enemies and those who oppress us? How can you form that into a habit for yourself without becoming bitter?
- Where do we go from here to help promote harmony among all God's people?

A Walk for Independence Day
(July 4)

Traditionally, colorings are to be Red, White, or Green if decorating around the Labyrinth, depending on how the occasion is celebrated: Martyrs, servants, or general thanksgivings.

Independence Day commemorates the day the U.S. founding fathers declared that the Thirteen Colonies were no longer subject to Great Britain and were now united, free, and independent states.

Preparing before the Labyrinth

Sitting or standing, take a moment of quiet contemplation and then pray:

"You have heard that it was said, 'You shall love your neighbor and hate your enemy.' But I say to you, Love your enemies and pray for those who persecute you, so that you may be children of your Father in heaven; for He makes His sun rise on the evil and on the good, and sends rain on the righteous and on the unrighteous. For if you love those who love you, what reward do you have? Do not even the tax collectors do the same? And if you greet only your brothers and sisters, what more are you doing than others? Do not even the Gentiles do the same? Be perfect, therefore, as your heavenly Father is perfect. *(Matthew 5:43–48)*

Almighty Ruler of Heaven and Earth, by whose grace this country was founded on the bases of life, liberty, and the pursuit of happiness, I praise You for this land. Bless us with peace and prosperity and fill us with the willingness to share our abundance with those in need. Strengthen our resolve to keep faithful to the concepts of freedom and welcoming the stranger upon which this nation was built. Teach us continued and increasing justice, compassion, and peace. *Amen.*

The Labyrinth

Begin the Labyrinth as is most expedient for that space, and if possible, sing or listen to a patriotic hymn from the hymnal or similar thematically appropriate music. In the Labyrinth, focus on praying or repeating phrases like:

> Guide us to love and serve You, and help us make this country one that resembles your Kingdom. Thank You for those who have struggled for justice and peace.

The Procession from Labyrinth into the World

> For the Lord your God is God of gods and Lord of lords, the great God, mighty and awesome, who is not partial and takes no bribe, who executes justice for the orphan and the widow, and who loves the strangers, providing them food and clothing. As you shall fear the Lord your God; Him alone you shall worship; to Him you shall hold fast, and by His name you shall swear. He is your praise; He is your God, who has done for you these great and awesome things that your own eyes have seen. *(Deuteronomy 10:17–21)*

Great King of Heaven and Earth, whose service is perfect freedom, liberate my heart and mind that I might serve You and this nation. Strengthen my faith so that I can be more compassionate and be a true peacemaker, especially with those I perceive to be my enemies. Empower me to be humble and true to You and to this land that we may fulfill our potential of blessing all the people of the world. In your Holy Name I pray. *Amen.*

Reflections from the Labyrinth

If we are to seek God in any country, we must first seek God in our own hearts. Most countries were founded on principles of freedom and justice, but many, if not all, fall short of their own ideals. Deuteronomy reminds us that "You shall also love the stranger, for you were strangers in the land of Egypt." Following this commandment, our nation should welcome strangers, as many of our ancestors were strangers when they arrived here, willingly or not. Let us strive to channel our faith—and not our fear—as people searching for better lives come to our soil.

Questions to ask yourself

- In what ways can you make this country better and truly honor God?

- How can you respect other people's faith if you do not understand your own?

- Why would someone fear the stranger coming to our land if that person's trust is in God?

A Walk for Columbus/Indigenous People's Day (second Monday in October)

This holiday is beyond ecclesiastical tradition, so colorings should be White if decorating around the Labyrinth.

Christopher Columbus and other explorers who landed in the Americas in the late fifteenth century onward made great discoveries, but they failed in many ways to treat indigenous Americans with dignity and compassion. Columbus Day/Indigenous People's Day is a reminder that every human being, regardless of race, gender, and creed, is created in God's blessed image and is worthy of love, respect, and equal treatment.

Preparing before the Labyrinth

Sitting or standing, take a moment of quiet contemplation and then pray:

Great Chief who rules all the tribes of heaven and earth, I celebrate this day of remembrance. For some, this day is a celebration of discovery and opening of new realms and resources. For others, it is a day of mourning for the loss of sovereignty and peace. Unite us under the banner of your Kingdom, so that peace and kindness prevail and every rift among us is healed under your divine love. Let us sing your praises with many voices in our many languages, each praising you in a special and faithful way. Bind us together, Sovereign King of the Universe, so that we all may remember that we are loved and chosen by you.

The Labyrinth

Begin the Labyrinth as is most expedient for that space, and if possible, sing or listen to the hymn or similar thematically appropriate music. Consider a repeated prayer such as:

Open my heart to all people, Lord. Take away my fear, arrogance, and pride so that your Love conquers all.

ROBERT J. F. ELSNER

The Procession from Labyrinth into the World

Let me give thanks to You, loving God, and praise your name in this free land. Empower me to aid the cause of justice. Embolden me to honor all traditions of the peoples who make this place their home. Write your laws in my heart, and in the hearts of all people, so that we may truly come together as one country, united in love, that reflects your kingdom. Let our ever-shining seas and fertile lands praise your name and may fear and hunger be but a memory. *Amen.*

Reflections from the Labyrinth

This is a holiday that many people across the political spectrum are passionate about. In the labyrinth, alone with God, it is important to work through your own feelings and to seek out understanding and tolerance of other perspectives. If our history is crowded by fear and desperate pride, we cannot see God in the frame of history, and this causes us to lose opportunities to center ourselves on Him. Abraham Lincoln is given credit for the quote: "Sir, my concern is not whether God is on our side; my greatest concern is to be on God's side, for God is always right."[3] I encourage you to do the same.

Questions to ask yourself

- Can you celebrate both the indigenous cultures of this land and the migrants from Europe and the rest of the world?

- Do the sins of our forebearers make us lesser people in God's eyes?

- Where does pride in our own heritage rob others of theirs and diminish God's creation of us all?

---

3. Carpenter, F.B. (1867) *Six Months in the White House with Abraham Lincoln.* Hurd and Houghton. As cited by: *https://www.politifact.com/factchecks/2008/sep/12/sarah-palin/not-far-from-lincolns-sentiment/*

A Walk for Thanksgiving Day
(fourth Thursday in November)

Traditionally, colorings are to be Green if decorating around the Labyrinth.

Thanksgiving is a holiday of remembrance of hospitality and a celebration of the bounty of the earth. It is a celebration of humility as well as generosity.

Preparing before the Labyrinth

Sitting or standing, take a moment of quiet contemplation and then read Psalm 100 and pray:

> Be joyful in the Lord, all you lands; *serve the Lord with gladness and come before his presence with a song.
>
> Know this: The Lord Himself is God; * He himself has made us, and we are His; we are his people and the sheep of His pasture.
>
> Enter His gates with thanksgiving; go into His courts with praise; * give thanks to Him and call upon His Name.
>
> For the Lord is good; His mercy is everlasting; * and His faithfulness endures from age to age.

Rejoice, starry heavens, crystal seas, and fruitful Earth, for the Lord has made you and shown great love for you. God has promised plenty to those who trust in Him, and this land has been blessed richly. Thank You, Lord of all, for what you have given me. Guide my mind to clearly see that all is from your bounty and not of my own merit. Let me revel in your blessings, even when they seem scarce. Let me remember that this early life is short, and I need to be quick to bless others so that they also give thanks to You and praise your name.

The Labyrinth

Begin the Labyrinth as is most expedient for that space, and if possible, sing or listen to the hymn or similar thematically appropriate music. Consider a repeated prayer such as:

Thank you, Heavenly Ruler, for all that I have. Help me to see the riches you shower upon me.

The Procession from Labyrinth into the World

When they found him on the other side of the sea, they said to him, "Rabbi, when did you come here?" Jesus answered them, "Very truly, I tell you, you are looking for me, not because you saw signs, but because you ate your fill of the loaves. Do not work for the food that perishes, but for the food that endures for eternal life, which the Son of Man will give you. For it is on him that God the Father has set his seal." Then they said to him, "What must we do to perform the works of God?" Jesus answered them, "This is the work of God, that you believe in him whom He has sent." So they said to him, "What sign are you going to give us then, so that we may see it and believe you? What work are you performing? Our ancestors ate the manna in the wilderness; as it is written, 'He gave them bread from heaven to eat.'" Then Jesus said to them, "Very truly, I tell you, it was not Moses who gave you the bread from heaven, but it is my Father who gives you the true bread from heaven. For the bread of God is that which comes down from heaven and gives life to the world." They said to him, "Sir, give us this bread always." Jesus said to them, "I am the bread of life. Whoever comes to me will never be hungry, and whoever believes in me will never be thirsty. (*John 6:25-35*)

Thank You, Founder of all Feasts, for the many blessings I have received from your hands. Remind me always that all comes from your grace, not the sweat of my brow. Enlighten my heart to remember those less fortunate than me, so that I can be a blessing to them in your name. Fill me with love and kindness that I may truly be in your image. *Amen.*

Reflections from the Labyrinth

On the first Thanksgiving immigrants who came to America seeking religious and economic liberty were saved from starvation by the generosity of indigenous people. Thanksgiving is therefore an opportunity for us to avoid overindulging and to share and provide for those who cannot provide for themselves. As Israel sought help from Egypt during famine, we should strive to be hospitable to others on Thanksgiving and every day thereafter.

Questions to ask yourself

- Can you truly be thankful on this day without recognizing that all comes as blessings from God?

- How do we rectify poverty and hunger in a world where so much food goes to waste every day? What should we be doing about such inequity and injustice?

- Do you thank God for your food, or merely recite a grace taught to you (if even that)?

- Should each meal remind you of Communion and the celebration of the Eucharist?

A Walk for President's Day
(Third Monday in February)

Traditionally, colorings are to be Green if decorating around the Labyrinth.

Our leaders are responsible for maintaining the freedoms and rights of all people. The demands of the job are numerous, difficult, and deserving of prayer, no matter who is in the office.

Preparing before the Labyrinth

Sitting or standing, take a moment of quiet contemplation and then pray:

> Where there is no guidance, a people falls, but in an abundance of counselors there is safety. *(Proverbs 11:14)*

> With upright heart he shepherded them and guided them with his skillful hand. *(Psalm 78:72)*

> "It shall not be so among you. But whoever would be great among you must be your servant, and whoever would be first among you must be your slave, even as the Son of Man came not to be served but to serve, and to give his life as a ransom for many." *(Matthew 20:26–28)*

O Lord our Governor, whose glory is in every nation in the world. Thank You for the life and leadership of all presidents of this country. I beseech you to keep this nation in your merciful care, and to inspire all who lead to be guided by your grace and blessings. Grant to the President of the United States—and to all in authority—wisdom and strength to know and to do your will. Fill the current and all future leaders with humility, honesty, integrity, and a love of truth and righteousness. Surround them all with the confidence of your love, so that they do not define their rule with fear, hatred, or persecution. Remind them that You are the ultimate authority under whose kingship they preside. I pray this in the name of Jesus Christ our Lord, who lives and reigns with You and the Holy Spirit, one God, world without end. Amen.

The Labyrinth

Begin the Labyrinth as is most expedient for that space. At the center of the Labyrinth, focus on what leadership means to this country and the world: Consider a repeated prayer such as:

> O Lord, guide and defend our rulers and mercifully hear us when we call upon thee.

The Procession from Labyrinth into the World

> For by the grace given to me I say to everyone among you not to think of himself more highly than he ought to think, but to think with sober judgment, each according to the measure of faith that God has assigned. For as in one body we have many members, and the members do not all have the same function, so we, though many, are one body in Christ, and individually members one of another. Having gifts that differ according to the grace given to us, let us use them: if prophecy, in proportion to our faith; if service, in our serving; the one who teaches, in his teaching; the one who exhorts, in his exhortation; the one who contributes, in generosity; the one who leads, with zeal; the one who does acts of mercy, with cheerfulness. *(Romans 12:3–8)*

Bless us all, O Lord, your willing and loving servants. We thank You for the social orders that put the most able in place to lead and ask for your forgiveness and corrections when we have failed in that task. Bless the President of this nation, and all others in authority, so that peace and harmony prevail and that all are respected as your beloved children. Heal the brokenhearted across all political spectrums and remind us all that we are under your Kingship. *Amen.*

ROBERT J. F. ELSNER

Reflections from the Labyrinth

Several times in the Book of Judges we see the phrase: "In those days there was no king in Israel; everyone did what was right in his own eyes" *(Judges 21:25)*. While this is a reference to Israel's forgetfulness of God's sovereignty, it was also a statement that the rulers of all countries must be willing to humble themselves before God and ask for forgiveness. We honor those who have led this country, even when they failed in areas, because they still served some purpose in God's plan for us all.

Questions to ask yourself

- Why should we pray for a particular person who is in power? When you pray for the President, is it to change that person's mind, or to ask God to guide and strengthen them?

- Why might God allow people into office who do not hold the same views as we do?

- Does that mean that they are here to punish us for something?

- When is it important that, irrespective of the President's faith, we pray for that President?

- .How can prayer directly help us, even if it does not change a political reality at the moment?

A Walk for Memorial Day
(Last Monday of May)

Traditionally, colorings are to be Red if decorating around the Labyrinth.
Memorial Day commemorates those who lost their lives in service to their country, or who served and have since died.

Preparing before the Labyrinth

Sitting or standing, take a moment of quiet contemplation and then pray:

> This is my commandment, that you love one another as I have loved you. Greater love has no one than this, that someone lay down his life for his friends. You are my friends if you do what I command you. No longer do I call you servants, for the servant does not know what his master is doing; but I have called you friends, for all that I have heard from my Father I have made known to you. You did not choose me, but I chose you and appointed you that you should go and bear fruit and that your fruit should abide, so that whatever you ask the Father in my name, he may give it to you. These things I command you, so that you will love one another. *(John 15:12-17)*

Commander of all the forces of Heaven, who created and rules the Universe, You have blessed the peacemakers. I praise You this day as I remember those who have given their lives in service to their country. Hold their souls in the palm of your hand, forgiving them of any sins and cherishing their selflessness and bravery to serve. You chose them, Lord, even if they did not choose You. Let light perpetual shine on them and those who loved them. Glory to You, Lord of all, who remembers those widowed and orphaned by wars and catastrophes and gives them comfort. *Amen.*

The Labyrinth

Begin the Labyrinth as is most expedient for that space. At the center of the Labyrinth, focus on remembering the sacrifices of those fallen in service to their country. Consider a repeated prayer such as:

Blessed are the peacemakers and those who fought for causes they thought just. Give peace in our time.

The Procession from Labyrinth into the World

Blessed is the nation whose God is the LORD, the people whom He has chosen as His heritage! The LORD looks down from heaven; He sees all the children of man; from where He sits enthroned He looks out on all the inhabitants of the earth, He who fashions the hearts of them all and observes all their deeds. The king is not saved by his great army; a warrior is not delivered by his great strength. The war horse is a false hope for salvation, and by its great might it cannot rescue. Behold, the eye of the LORD is on those who fear Him, on those who hope in His steadfast love, that He may deliver their soul from death and keep them alive in famine. Our soul waits for the LORD; He is our help and our shield. For our heart is glad in Him, because we trust in His holy name. Let your steadfast love, O LORD, be upon us, even as we hope in you. *(Psalm 33:12-22)*

Lord of all, by whose kindness peace is established. We, your children, have rebelled against You and brought war, corruption, and injustice to the earth. I praise You and thank You, Almighty God, for the lives of those women and men who have served their country and lain down their lives in defense of justice and freedom. Comfort those who have survived the loss of these defenders of freedom and bless those now serving to have the strength and bravery to complete their tasks, and the wisdom to avoid death when possible. While I see that death is not the end, Lord, I know that it is a great fear among your people. Strengthen our faith more than our arms, O God, that our trust is always in You. *Amen.*

Reflections from the Labyrinth

Memorial Day was instituted to commemorate the sacrifices of the soldiers who died during the Civil War. At that time, five thousand people helped decorate the graves of the more than 20,000 Union and Confederate soldiers who were buried there. This practice was inspired by a gathering in Charleston, South Carolina in May 1865, when formerly enslaved people came together to pay tribute to the Union troops who fought for their freedom. Throughout history we have sung the songs of heroes and those who have fought and died. Memorial Day should be an opportunity to continue this rich tradition and a time to pray for peace and the end of war.

Questions to ask yourself

- How do we honor those who gave their lives for ideals in which they believed?

- Do we remember the innocent casualties who lost their lives in wars and catastrophes?

- How can we change our prayer lives so that we become peacemakers and fully glorify God?

A Walk for Veteran's Day
(November 11th)

Traditionally, colorings are to be Green if decorating around the Labyrinth.

Veteran's Day is a celebration of the lives of those who have served or are serving in the military.

Preparing before the Labyrinth

Sitting or standing, take a moment of quiet contemplation and then pray:

> And he said, The LORD is my rock and my fortress and my deliverer; My God, my rock, in whom I take refuge; My shield and the horn of my salvation, my stronghold and my refuge; My savior, Thou dost save me from violence. I call upon the LORD, who is worthy to be praised; And I am saved from my enemies. (*2 Samuel 22:2–4*)

Author of Life, I praise You and glorify your name for blessing us with men and women who have served in the armed forces to protect this nation. Let me appreciate the sacrifices of those who serve and those whose service is complete. Help me to see that their work is and has been in the pursuit of peace and justice.

The Labyrinth

Begin the Labyrinth as is most expedient for that space, and if possible, sing or listen to the hymn "America the Beautiful," "God of our Fathers," "Almighty Father, Strong to save," or similar thematically appropriate music. At the center of the Labyrinth, focus on those who have served their country and may have scars, visible and invisible. During the labyrinth journey, consider a repeated prayer such as:
For veterans:

> The LORD is my rock, my fortress and my deliverer; my God is my rock, in whom I take refuge, my shield and the horn of my salvation, my stronghold. (*Psalm 18:2*)

For those actively serving:

> For those who defend our Country, I give thanks. For those who will sacrifice, I ask Comfort.

The Procession from Labyrinth into the World

> We ought always to thank God for you, brothers and sisters, and rightly so, because your faith is growing more and more, and the love all of you have for one another is increasing. Therefore, among God's churches, we boast about your perseverance and faith in all the persecutions and trials you are enduring. *(2 Thessalonians 1:3–4)*

Ruler of Heaven and Earth, whose angels have charge over us to bring us messages of truth, You have given us wisdom and rational minds to think through all things. Help us to honor those who serve to defend this country, so that they might show wisdom, compassion, and mercy as they make hard decisions. Let the strength of their hearts be even greater than the strength of their arms. Pour into them faith and integrity so that they do not lose their way. Bind up and heal all wounds of body, mind, and soul that may trouble those who have served. Enfold us all in your love that we may see the end to all war and violence, joining hands to worship you throughout all ages. *Amen.*

Reflections from the Labyrinth

It is a good and honorable thing to serve your fellow humans and your country. On this day we remember those who put on uniforms or took oaths of office and conduct to defend the rights of other people, even at risk to their own lives. Many veterans have scars that are visible, and many have scars that none can see except for God. The mental health issues faced by those who have been in harm's way are innumerable and should engender compassion and kindness in us.

Questions to ask yourself

- What are the spiritual battles veterans may face?
- How can I help serve those who have served?
- Why do many veterans not seek out help for their mental, emotional, or spiritual wounds?
- How can honoring our veterans help ensure peace in the world?

BIBLIOGRAPHY

Candolini, G. (2003). *Labyrinths: Walking toward the center*. Crossroad Publishing.

Danaher J. P. (2011). *Contemplative prayer: a theology for the twenty-first century*. Cascade Books.

Episcopal Church. (1979). *The Book of Common Prayer and Administration of the Sacraments and Other Rites and Ceremonies of the Church: together with the Psalter or Psalms of David: according to the use of the Episcopal Church*. Church Hymnal Corp.

Fontana D. (2001). *The secret language of symbols: a visual key to symbols and their meanings*. Chronicle Books.

Furr, G.A., & Price, M. (1998). *The Dialog of Worship: Creating Space for Revelation and Response*. Smith & Helwys Publishing.

Heuertz P. (2010). *Pilgrimage of a soul: contemplative spirituality for the active life*. IVP Books.

Kavanaugh, K. (2003). Contemplation and the stream of consciousness. In K.J. Egan (Ed.), *Carmelite Prayer: A tradition for the 21ˢᵗ century*. Paulist Press.

Keating, T. (1978). Contemplative prayer in Christian tradition. In T. Keating, M.B. Pennington, and T.E. Clark (Eds). *Finding Grace at the Center*. Petersham, MA: St. Bede's Publications.

McLuhan M. (1964). *Understanding media: the extensions of man (6ᵗʰ printing)*. McGraw-Hill.

Paintner C. V. & Wynkoop L. (2008). *Lectio divina: contemplative awakening and awareness*. Paulist Press.

Pennington, M.B. (1982). *Centering Prayer: Renewing an ancient Christian prayer form*. Doubleday.

Pennington, M.B. (1985). Centering Prayer. In T. Keating, M.B. Pennington, and T.E. Clark (Eds). *Finding Grace at the Center*. St. Bede's Publications.

Peterson E. H. (1993). *The contemplative pastor : returning to the art of spiritual direction*. Wm. B. Eerdmans Pub.

Rule of Benedict, (prologue 1) accessed at: https://ccel.org/ccel/benedict/rule/rule.ii.html

Wallraff M., Seidel Menchi, S. & von Greyerz, K. (2016). *Basel 1516: Erasmus' edition of the New Testament*. Mohr Siebeck.

Welch, S. (2010). *Walking the labyrinth: a spiritual and practical guide*. Canterbury Press.

Wright, C.M. (2001). *The Maze and the Warrior: Symbols in architecture, theology, and music*. Harvard University Press.